T0023118

365 WAYS TO SAVE THE PLANET

365 WAYS
TO SAVE THE PLANET

NERGIZ DE BAERE

First published in Great Britain by John Murray Learning in 2022
An imprint of John Murray Press
A division of Hodder & Stoughton Ltd.
An Hachette UK company

1

Copyright © Nergiz De Baere 2022

A CIP catalogue record for this title is available from the British Library

Hardback ISBN 978 1 52939 741 3
eBook ISBN 978 1 52939 740 6

Typeset by KnowledgeWorks Global Ltd.

Printed and bound in Great Britain by Clays Ltd, Elcograf S.p.A.

John Murray Press policy is to use papers that are natural, renewable and
recyclable products and made from wood grown in sustainable forests.
The logging and manufacturing processes are expected to conform to the
environmental regulations of the country of origin.

John Murray Press
Carmelite House
50 Victoria Embankment
London EC4Y 0DZ

www.johnmurraypress.co.uk

CONTENTS

ABOUT THE AUTHOR

Nergiz De Baere is an Azerbaijani-Belgian activist, author, friend, daughter, and fellow human. She created the popular Instagram page Chicks for Climate (@chicksforclimate) where she shares educational posts about feminism and environmentalism with 400k+ community members. She was born in Kenya and raised in London, Norway, and Azerbaijan, before receiving a degree in Economics from Barnard College in New York City. She can usually be found hugging trees in the leafy suburbs of West London where she currently lives.

INTRODUCTION

I was nine years old when I attended my first protest. It was November 2005, and the parliamentary elections of Azerbaijan had just been held, with dubious results. I shouted 'Resign', 'Freedom', 'Say no to corruption, say yes to democracy' with one fist in the air and one tightly gripped around the waistband of my new jeans I was still growing into.

The rally was inspired by Ukraine's Orange Revolution of 2004–5: protestors were carrying orange flags and wearing orange clothing. My grandma bought me an orange inflatable lion to hold, which only added to my excitement about the whole event. The rally in Victory Square started off peacefully, joyfully even. But after a couple of hours, sensing there would be a police crackdown, my grandma took me home.

My grandparents never hid hard truths from me. I recall a sobering moment the day after the protest, watching the news, when I saw a photograph of a woman with blood all over her face. She was just steps away from where I had been standing in the square.

As a nine-year-old, I had no idea of the full gravity and meaning of the words I was shouting that day, but I understood that I was shouting to achieve something important. I could sense the passion from the adults around me, and I understand now that I was sensing an urgency to fight for a better world, to fight for justice.

Though we failed to obtain the justice we wanted that day, and though the experience left me with a keen sense of the ugly realities of the world, I am still moved by the hope and optimism I felt in that sea of orange. And though I now feel powerless to help further that cause, the experience motivated me to use the power I do have to advocate for justice and better the world in other ways.

After an unseasonably hot day in London in February 2019, I decided to use my power to start an Instagram account that would raise awareness and educate people about the climate crisis and other social issues. I read countless academic articles and news stories and then translated my learnings into accessible and easy-to-read posts that I published almost every day. Unexpectedly, the page amassed a few hundred thousand followers.

This book is the culmination of everything I've learned, and my promise to you is that it will give you the tools, encouragement and knowledge you need to be an outstanding advocate for our planet and all who live on it.

We need to understand the Earth and its complexities if we are to be motivated to make positive change. That's why this book will give you the knowledge you need to be motivated, inspired and poised to take action on the right things.

Saving the planet isn't only about taking action. It's also about learning and awareness, and about healing and renewing our relationship with nature. The capitalist system we live in doesn't incentivize consideration for the environment because there's no monetary gain for doing so. To continue living on this planet, we must cultivate ecological empathy, and that includes changing the exploitative system that abuses nature and vulnerable people.

You will be given the tools to be a planetary advocate on all fronts, from wide-reaching system change to smaller but no less impactful community change.

You'll see that I mention voting and speaking to your local politicians very regularly throughout the whole book. I do this to emphasize the importance of advocacy and political involvement in the fight to stop the climate crisis. We're in this mess because the system we live in has allowed for it, and we can't solve the problem of climate destruction without making our voices and the voices of the marginalized heard in government.

We'll talk about some difficult and sobering issues, but my purpose is not to make you lose hope. Talking honestly about tough issues is important, particularly for the purposes of jolting us into action and giving us even more motivation and urgency to change the status quo.

This book will inspire you to take action, but your positive impact will be multiplied if you involve yourself in your community. The strength of humanity lies in the strength of our communities – no one can save the planet and change the system alone. What's more, in times of despair and difficulty, being able to vent to people and hug loved ones is absolutely priceless.

I am honoured that you have made the decision to join planet and people in the fight for justice. While you're on this journey, remember that this is not about being perfect, and that even if you read this book end to end, there will still be more to do. Our success lies in asking ourselves what these things are, and hopefully this book will serve as a launchpad for you to have these conversations with yourself and your community.

I dedicate this book to the thousands of activists around the world who have given their lives and freedoms to fight for justice, to the voiceless, to the powerless, and to future generations who deserve nothing less than to inherit a healthy planet.

CHAPTER 1

THE BASICS

1   How did we get here?

For thousands of years, humans have been burning things to create energy. Our ancestors lit fires from wood and later discovered substances like petroleum and coal which burn longer and stronger. After the kerosene (oil) lamp was invented in the nineteenth century, the oil rush began, which ushered in a new age of human prosperity.

Industrialization and combustion using fossil fuels have dramatically changed the lives of humans. As a species, we're living longer than ever, we're richer than ever. Extreme poverty, child mortality, and deaths from war and disease are at historic lows.

But our love of 'black gold' and its ability to keep us warm, fed and rich has come at a huge cost to the planet and its inhabitants, non-human as well as human. We've used our newfound power given to us by fossil fuels to exploit other natural 'resources' such as forests, animals, water and minerals. We have built our societies around the exploitation of nature, and by doing so, are emitting billions of tonnes of greenhouse gas emissions into the atmosphere. And now, the balance of nature has been disrupted.

Our planet's stable weather patterns and temperatures have been shifting because we've burned too many of our resources too quickly. To make matters worse, the system we live in does not allow for equal enjoyment of these resources, which means the world's most vulnerable people have missed out on the benefits and are now stuck with dire environmental consequences.

2   What is the greenhouse effect?

The greenhouse effect keeps our planet warm enough for life to exist. Earth has an atmosphere that traps heat from the Sun, keeping us warm even at night when the Sun's heat is on the other side of the planet. Without greenhouse gases in our atmosphere, Earth would be 33 degrees Celsius cooler.[1]

The atmosphere functions like the roof of a greenhouse, except there aren't glass panels hovering above Earth. Greenhouse gases such as carbon dioxide, methane and nitrous oxide serve this function instead, trapping heat from the Sun. These gases naturally occur in our atmosphere, and they've helped to create a favourable environment for human, animal and plant life to thrive.

But since the Industrial Revolution (roughly 1760–1840), humans have been adding more of these gases to the atmosphere at an extremely high rate. The more of these gases we emit into the atmosphere, the greater the warming effect on the planet.

Because humans emit so many greenhouse gases through our activities, we've warmed the planet enough to trigger unpredictable weather patterns and rapidly melting ice caps.

3   What are the different greenhouse gases?

Our atmosphere is a delicate balance of different chemicals and gases that interact to make life on Earth possible. It's important to know what the different greenhouse gases are so we can understand how they warm the planet.

Carbon dioxide is the most worrisome greenhouse gas and is responsible for most of the global warming effect. It's not the most powerful greenhouse gas, but it's dangerous because there is so much of it being emitted through burning oil, natural gas and coal. Carbon dioxide absorbs heat energy from the Sun and re-emits that heat back into the atmosphere.[2] More carbon dioxide in the atmosphere means more heat energy being absorbed and emitted.

Methane is another greenhouse gas and is 25 times more powerful at heating the atmosphere than carbon dioxide.[3] It's emitted not only when fossil fuels are burned but also when organic matter decomposes without oxygen. Cow burps and decaying organic waste in landfills are the two big contributors to excess methane in the atmosphere.

Nitrous oxide is 298 times more potent at warming than carbon dioxide and is mainly released from agricultural activities.[4]

Fluorinated gases – which are the most potent but least common greenhouse gases in the atmosphere – are synthetic and most commonly used in aerosol cans and refrigeration.

4   What's the difference between the climate crisis and climate change?

For the past few years, the language used to describe human-influenced environmental disasters has changed to reflect the scale of the emergency we're facing. At first, 'global warming' or 'climate change' were used interchangeably to describe the changes scientists were observing in the planet's average temperature.

Even though awareness around climate change has persisted for decades, our leaders have failed to act at every turn, which has resulted in more natural disasters and extreme weather events. The term 'climate crisis' is more appropriate to describe the seriousness of the damage that has been done over the past century.

Climate change is normally used to describe the scientific and meteorological effects of human activities. The threats and dangers that are faced because of climate change are described as the climate crisis.

5   Deforestation: the planet killer

Trees are incredible. They give us oxygen, they clean our soil, they provide homes for birds and insects, and they store huge amounts of carbon. They're constantly and silently working to make our planet a healthier, safer and more beautiful place.

Human ingenuity has found multiple uses for trees beyond the safety and oxygen they provide for us. We use wood from trees for paper, toilet roll, cigarette filters, paper bags, flooring and countless other products. Although trees have brought us many conveniences, our ability to place a monetary value on them means their non-monetary benefits have been forgotten. When we cut them down, we deprive our planet and its wildlife of essential parts of the ecosystem – all so we can make money.

Deforestation is responsible for around 19 per cent of global greenhouse gas emissions.[5] Let's put into perspective how much forest is cut down to accommodate our demand for products that come from trees.

Consider that an area the size of the landmass of the UK is deforested every year to meet the country's demand for the following products:

- cocoa
- palm oil
- paper
- rubber
- soy
- timber
- beef
- leather.[6]

Even worse, half of the world's tropical deforestation is illegal.[7] Cutting trees to make room or to sell wood is a quick way to make lots of money, so there are always people willing to do this illegally.

If we keep removing trees at an unsustainable rate, we remove the tools life has created to keep our air clean and our atmosphere cool enough to support us. We leave ourselves incredibly vulnerable to heatwaves, dirty air and less diversity of wildlife in our ecosystems. Ending deforestation is one of the quickest and most effective ways to slow down climate change.

According to a UN report, Indigenous peoples are by far the best protectors of forests. Deforestation rates are up to 50 per cent lower in Indigenous territories than anywhere else.[8] If you want to support ending deforestation, donate to a non-profit organization protecting Indigenous rights.

6   Where do all our emissions really come from?

Before understanding how you can save the planet, you should first understand where the biggest sources of greenhouse gases are found.[9]

The biggest source of emissions globally by far is the burning of fossil fuels for energy to propel the global economy.

We make a lot of stuff, and making stuff needs energy. Industry is responsible for around 25 per cent of greenhouse gas emissions globally, mostly for creating iron and steel, pharmaceuticals and fertilizers, extracting oil and gas, mining and quarrying, and manufacturing textiles and cars.

Humans also travel a lot, and most modern transport equipment is based on the combustion engine, which emits greenhouse gases. The transport sector emits around 16 per cent of global emissions. This includes burning petrol and diesel for cars, buses, trucks, boats and planes.

We also live in houses and work in offices that need energy for heating, cooling, cooking and lighting. Producing electricity for these activities is responsible for around 17 per cent of global emissions.

The rest of the emissions from energy are unallocated or escape during energy production. All in all, energy is responsible for around 76 per cent of global emissions.

The next biggest emitter of greenhouse gases after energy is agriculture, forestry and land use. This is responsible for 18.4 per cent of greenhouse gases, and includes rearing cows and sheep, using synthetic fertilizers on soils, cultivating rice, burning crops, deforestation and cropland degradation.

We'll talk about a few of these in the upcoming sections, including how we can reduce some of the emissions associated with them.

7 The evidence that climate change is caused by humans

The consensus in the scientific community is that climate change is caused by humans. Scientists have observed warming trends in the atmosphere over the past century and have concluded that warming has happened too fast to be caused naturally.

The concentrations of greenhouse gases in the atmosphere have increased every year since the Industrial Revolution. There is 40 per cent more carbon dioxide, 150 per cent more methane and 20 per cent more nitrous dioxide in the atmosphere now than in pre-industrial times.

For around 10,000 years, carbon dioxide concentrations in the atmosphere stayed stable at around 260 parts per million.[10] As of 2022, levels of carbon dioxide in the atmosphere are at around 417 parts per million,[11] because humans are releasing billions of tonnes of carbon dioxide into the atmosphere every year.

Using basic physics, we know that carbon dioxide absorbs heat and that more carbon dioxide in the atmosphere means global warming.

8 Have we always known climate change would happen?

As far back as 1938, scientists connected carbon dioxide increases in the atmosphere to global warming.[12] In 1979, the First World Climate Conference was held, bringing together scientists from around the world in what could have been a turning point for stopping global warming. Even though climate conferences have been held for decades, many obstacles have stood in the way of swift climate action, mostly to do with corporate self-interest and profit-making. Two years earlier, in 1977, oil companies had been preparing their own version of science to do everything possible to stop any progress on climate action, in order to protect their own profits.[13]

From that time on, a decades-long lobbying operation began, spearheaded by major oil companies, to discourage carbon dioxide regulation in government and to discredit scientists who studied climate change. These companies also ran PR campaigns to shift the blame of climate change onto the individual rather than themselves.

So yes, we've pretty much always known climate change would happen, and this crisis is not an accident. It's the result of decades of misinformation, corruption and unbridled capitalism, the consequences of which will now affect the world's most vulnerable people.

9   The Paris Climate Accords

The Paris Agreement, often known as the Paris Climate Accords, was signed in 2015, and brought together 196 countries in an agreement to limit global warming to under 2 degrees Celsius, preferably 1.5 degrees Celsius. Although there isn't an international court set up to make sure countries make good on their pledges, the agreement is technically legally binding.

Each participating country is required to submit plans for how it is going to decrease greenhouse gas emissions, called nationally determined contributions (NDCs). The agreement recognizes that countries that contribute the least to climate change suffer the most from its effects, and includes a plan for richer countries to provide financial assistance to these countries.

Current climate pledges made at the Paris Climate Accords in 2015 by the world's richest countries mean global warming is set to reach 2.4 degrees Celsius.[14]

Politicians need to treat this crisis like the emergency it is. Pledges are a step in the right direction, but things are moving too slowly, and the most disadvantaged in our societies are set to bear the consequences.

10   Will carbon capture save us?

So we know that climate change is caused by humans filling up the atmosphere with carbon dioxide. But what if we could remove the carbon dioxide at the same rate that we emit it?

Carbon capture technology does just that, and industry and governments around the world have been considering using this technology to curb emissions. Theoretically, this technology could capture the emissions from industrial and manufacturing facilities before they are emitted, or filter carbon dioxide out of the open air.

This sounds great, doesn't it? Except the technology is nowhere near ready to be rolled out on a big scale. Currently, carbon capture systems capture only around 0.1 per cent of annual global emissions.[15]

To be implemented on a big scale, carbon capture systems need vast amounts of materials and land, which means we're probably better off saving those resources and the emissions associated with building the technology.

Focusing on carbon capture as a credible solution for the climate crisis is a distraction from the urgent need for us to reduce emissions and transition to renewable energy.

11   What's the deal with geoengineering?

In 1991, the Mount Pinatubo volcano in the Philippines erupted, sending sulphur dioxide into the air. The gas reflected back the Sun's rays, cooling the planet by half a degree Celsius for almost two years.

Geoengineering technologies would work in a similar way, spraying the stratosphere with sun-reflecting chemicals to cool the planet. Like carbon capture technology, this superficially sounds like a great idea, but it's a pretty controversial issue.

Some argue that geoengineering will give countries an excuse not to reduce greenhouse gas emissions. There are also considerable unknown risks involved with tinkering with the planet's atmosphere – spraying sulphur dioxide into the air could potentially have catastrophic effects on weather patterns around the world.

Other scientists hold a different view, arguing that geoengineering should still be researched, even if it's never deployed, because it could prove useful to prevent the most catastrophic effects of climate change in the future.

Whatever your opinion on geoengineering, what is unanimously agreed upon in the scientific community is that we need to reduce emissions *now*.

12   What's in a carbon footprint?

In the early 2000s, British Petroleum (or BP) hired the advertising agency Ogilvy & Mather to promote the idea that climate change is the fault of individuals.[16, 17, 18, 19] That's right, an oil giant and the world's sixth largest polluter wanted you to know that climate change is your fault.

As part of this successful and misleading PR campaign, BP unveiled the 'personal carbon footprint' calculator, so people could calculate how much their individual actions contributed to heating the planet. This shifted the responsibility of climate change away from the oil giants, which have been lobbying against climate action for decades.

The term 'personal carbon footprint' is a red herring because this crisis was not created by individuals but by powerful corporations and interests that profit from emitting greenhouse gases. During the COVID-19 pandemic, when most of the world's population was confined to their homes and presumably slashed their personal carbon footprints, emissions dropped by only 6 per cent.[20]

Although we should all be mindful of how our own lifestyles contribute to climate change, it's also important to hold fossil fuel companies and polluting organizations to account for the damage they have knowingly done to our planet.

13 Is reaching net zero by 2050 realistic?

According to the UN, more than 130 countries have pledged to reach net-zero emissions by 2050, which means the countries' emissions would be the same as the amount removed from the atmosphere through carbon capture. If this is to be achieved, the global economy and the infrastructure of the energy system will need a complete transformation.

We will need innovations to make existing technology more energy efficient. We'll need to use renewable energy as our main source of energy, and to capture and store the greenhouse gases we still need to emit to keep economies going. We will also need to change some lifestyle choices to reduce unnecessary existing emissions.

Investments in these technologies and reductions in emissions are happening far too slowly to make 2050 a realistic goal to reach net-zero emissions. But if governments, companies and citizens all work together in the 2020s and move quickly, it is still possible.

14 When will really be 'too late'?

There's no way to avoid some of the consequences of unabated pollution and fossil fuel burning over the last century, but as of 2022, it's still not too late to avoid the very worst consequences if governments take emergency action. Every half a degree of warming avoided would have a huge impact on avoiding the worst of species loss and extreme weather events.

But let's imagine that everything carries on as usual – when will the crisis get out of control? The truth is, no one knows. This sort of global warming is unprecedented, and it's very difficult for scientists to predict what might happen on a planetary scale.

Some of the changes we're already seeing, such as sea levels rising, are irreversible. Once we cross the 1.5 degree Celsius threshold, the ability of plants, animals and ecosystems to adapt will be put to the test – and some simply won't survive. This threshold is so important because we just aren't sure what might happen beyond it.

It's already too late to avoid the climate crisis completely, but we can limit warming to avoid the worst effects and help the most vulnerable to adapt.

15   How much positive impact can I really have?

You picked up this book because you feel passionate about the fight to save our planet and the world's most vulnerable people. It's totally normal to feel a little helpless and wonder how much impact you can have as just one person. A crisis of this magnitude should be eliciting an emergency response from our governments and leaders, but everything seems to be going on business as usual, so you might feel alone or isolated in your panic.

First, understand that it's not the responsibility of one person to solve the entire climate crisis. However, it is the responsibility of those who are already aware to spread that awareness, and to do things that are within their control. We often underestimate how much impact we can have as individuals, but sometimes, simply leading by example is effective enough. For example, if you take trains to avoid flying, telling someone else to do the same thing might make them think twice the next time they fly. It might be a cliché but being the change you want to see in the world really works.

If you want to go deeper, think about where you have power and sway in your own life. Maybe it's in your friend group, your office or your local community. How can you use what you've learned (and will learn) about the climate crisis to inform others and help them take action? What are your unique strengths, and how can you use them to spread awareness and increase the sense of urgency?

You have more power than you think to make a difference. Start with your community and build from there.

16   Did individuals cause climate change?

In sustainability, the word 'we' is often used to describe human effects on the climate crisis. But is it *our* fault? Is the average person responsible for the demise of the planet, or are we just individuals trying to survive in a system not built by us?

The richest 1 per cent of people create almost double the emissions of the poorest half of the world.[21] Companies send lobbyists to try to persuade politicians against introducing regulations that might protect the planet and the consumer. People who historically contribute the least to global emissions (such as women, people on low incomes, Black and Indigenous communities) disproportionately bear the consequences of climate change. It's a broken system from the inside out.

The capitalist system we live in is inherently exploitative, and we can't opt out of it if we're born into it. So, as individuals, we're not necessarily at fault for the ways in which our collective actions have heated up the planet. However, we do have a responsibility to do our part to try to better our society and help leave this planet better than we found it.

17   How much has the Earth already heated up?

The Industrial Revolution that began in the UK replaced human labour with machines that increased productivity to levels never seen before. These machines used fossil fuels to power immense engines that did the work of hundreds of people in far less time.

The Industrial Revolution brought many (especially in the Global North) the comforts and conveniences of modern life, raising the standard of living, but at a huge cost to the planet. Burning fossil fuel resources at a fast rate fills up the atmosphere with greenhouse gases, which, as of 2021, has led to the warming of our planet by 1.1 degrees Celsius since 1850.[22]

Just one degree of warming in the average temperature of our planet has caused ancient glaciers to melt, increased the frequency of drought and extreme heat events, and affected natural systems that had been stable for millions of years.

Unless governments take extreme measures to curb the amount of fossil fuels burned, the planet will continue to warm, and these negative effects will only get worse.

18   What is the difference between 1.5 and 2 degrees Celsius of warming?

It's almost impossible to be able to feel a temperature difference of half a degree Celsius. But for average planetary temperatures, half a degree more of warming makes a huge difference. At 2 degrees Celsius, we will lose twice as many plant and animal species, and three times as many insect species. It'll mean 37 per cent of the world population will be exposed to extreme heat once every five years, compared to 14 per cent at 1.5 degrees.[23]

Limiting warming to 1.5 degrees Celsius will also significantly reduce the chances of extreme drought and water stress. It will mean hundreds of millions fewer vulnerable people being exposed to climate risks and experiencing poverty and destitution.

The Paris Climate Accords brought the world's countries together to pledge to keep warming to below 1.5 degrees Celsius, but it's not going to be easy. We must hold our leaders accountable to make good on this pledge – it's a matter of life and death for many millions of people around the world.

19   Who has climate change already affected?

Climate change has already affected almost everyone on the planet, but its worst effects are being felt by the most marginalized and vulnerable people:

- Island nations near the equator, from the Atlantic to the Pacific to the Indian Ocean, are already experiencing record flooding that is contaminating drinking water and coastal erosion that is threatening to swallow up their entire landmass.
- Wildfires have raged out of control in Siberia, Turkey, Australia, the United States and Greece.
- Heatwaves have already killed hundreds of people across Europe and North America.
- Climate change-fuelled droughts in Somalia have killed hundreds of thousands and forced others to leave their homes in search of water and pasture.

For some, climate change is a future, long-term threat. But for many others, the climate crisis is a present and menacing danger.

Richer people in richer countries have more resources to protect themselves from the negative effects of climate change. Climate change will only make existing inequalities and vulnerabilities worse, which is why it's so important we fix the system that makes people vulnerable in the first place.

20   Do we still have time to reverse the climate crisis?

If you keep up with climate news, you can probably relate to the feeling of getting lost in the never-ending cycle of distressing stories, doomscrolling until you lose hope completely.

It can be easy to become demoralized and think that it's too late and climate apocalypse is inevitable. But unless you're reading this in 2029, there's still time. While some form of climate change is inevitable and already happening, we can still avoid the worst consequences.

As of 2022, no country is on track to meet emission cuts proposed by the Paris Climate Accords to keep warming to below 1.5 degrees Celsius.[24] If the global economy carries on business as usual, we will cross the 1.5 degrees threshold in the early 2030s.[25] This means we have only a few years to make drastic and emergency changes to the global economy to keep warming below the threshold.

Countries need to immediately phase out coal, stop deforestation, speed up the switch to electric vehicles, encourage investment in renewables, and put measures in place to protect the most vulnerable from the effects of climate change that are already here. The climate crisis is urgent and dire, but the worst effects are not irreversible – yet.

21   What has already been done about climate change?

It's so important to keep hopeful in the face of a crisis of this magnitude. Hope is the fuel that keeps us fighting and protesting and helps us through the anxiety. So let's discuss a few of the actions governments have already taken to curb climate change.

We need to keep fossil fuels in the ground to curb emissions. At the UN Climate Change Conference in October 2021, 20 of the world's richest countries pledged to stop funding international fossil fuel projects by the end of 2022. Several countries also pledged to phase out coal power, which is essential to curbing emissions.

Investment in renewable energy has also been exploding globally, fuelled by improvements in technology and cost reductions. More public spending is now being invested in renewables than in fossil fuels.[26]

Countries like France, the Netherlands, Canada and Finland have made considerable investments in sustainable agriculture and reducing food waste, which have landed them on the top of the list of the Food Sustainability Index.[27]

The solutions are all available to us, and there are leaders who truly care about implementing them for the good of the future of the planet. We just need more action, from more countries, faster.

22   What is eco-anxiety?

You know that feeling you get when you read that the planet is burning and that species are going extinct and that air pollution deaths are rising and that some cities won't exist in a few years because of flooding? That's eco-anxiety, which is stress caused by worrying about the existential threat climate change poses for humanity and life on this planet.

For most of our existence, humans mainly only needed to worry about where our next meal was coming from, or whether a simple infection would kill us. Now we're forced to think much bigger, about the larger threat our economic activity poses to millions of animals and other human beings on this planet. Most of us who feel eco-anxiety aren't people who have much power – we're regular people who didn't ask to be born into an exploitative system.

This frustration and helplessness can manifest as eco-anxiety – which is not necessarily a mental health illness, but a healthy reaction to the magnitude of the problem of climate change.

To make matters worse, there are plenty of people already feeling the effects of climate change in the form of increased heatwaves and natural disasters. We can't forget about the implications of the climate crisis on mental health, especially on those who will feel the worst effects of a warming planet.

23   What is ecofeminism?

When I started @chicksforclimate on Instagram to raise awareness about climate change and women's issues, I never imagined it would have the reach it does today. I decided to choose these two topics because I found that the women in my circles tended to be a bit more worried and vocal about the climate crisis than the men. After doing plenty of research to prepare myself to post about these issues, I discovered that women, especially in the Global South, are also more likely to be adversely affected by climate change.[28]

Ecofeminism is the idea that the oppression of women and the destruction of nature are related and are inflicted by patriarchal capitalism and white supremacy.

In English, and in many other languages, we talk about 'Mother Nature', which implies that nature is feminine. If we live in a society that exploits and oppresses women, then it's not too far off the mark to conclude that the exploitation and oppression of nature is antifeminist.

Ecofeminism also suggests that dismantling the patriarchy is best for the planet and our society. Patriarchal thinking is all about dominance and exploitation, but we cannot and should not dominate and exploit a planet that keeps us alive. Instead, we should respect and value all life equally.

If you want to do some further reading on this topic, I highly recommend Ayana Elizabeth Johnson's *All We Can Save* (Penguin Random House, 2020) and Maria Mies and Vandana Shiva's *Ecofeminism* (Zed Books, 2014).

24   Is overpopulation the issue?

It's undeniable that there are lots of people on Earth. Humans are the most successful animal species – we've managed to increase our life expectancy by decades in the past few centuries and, as a result, we're everywhere. But are there too many of us for the planet to handle? The answer is simple: no.

The idea that overpopulation has contributed to climate change is not only wrong but often has racist implications.

The overpopulation argument shifts the blame onto countries which have high population growth rates, which are currently overwhelmingly in the continent of Africa.[29] These countries are not to blame for climate change – wealthy countries in the Global North have far higher energy consumption than countries in the Global South.

The reality is, we have more than enough resources for everyone to live sustainably. The rate at which these resources are consumed by higher-income countries is unsustainable, and there's a lot of wastage and inefficiency.

Consider this: if every human being on the planet lived as close together as those living in New York City, we could all fit into the state of Texas. Space is certainly not a problem.

There are plenty of resources to go around for everyone – *if* those resources are used efficiently. If we had cheap, green energy readily available, regenerative agriculture as the norm, ethical business practices in place everywhere, and no subsidies for fossil fuels, we wouldn't have a climate crisis *and* we could support a growing population.

25 If we stop burning all fossil fuels now, will climate change stop?

Let's imagine you could press a button and stop burning fossil fuels completely. What would happen? Well, the global economy is so dependent on fossil fuels that society would probably collapse. As of 2020, fossil fuels provided over 80 per cent of global energy.[30]

But societal collapse aside, would this stop climate change? The short answer is: not immediately.

There's a delayed effect in the carbon we've been emitting and how it gets translated to heat in the atmosphere. For example, the ocean takes longer to warm than the atmosphere, which means residual warming will still happen even after we stop burning fossil fuels.

That doesn't mean all hope is lost. We can still avoid having to deal with a global climate collapse if we reduce emissions to a manageable level. Reducing our emissions can still slow warming and give us time to adapt to a warmer planet.

26 Why aren't governments moving faster?

Rich countries' climate targets are still not enough to stop a climate crisis. Current climate pledges from these countries mean warming is set to reach 2.4 degrees Celsius by the end of the century, and we will emit almost twice as much in 2030 as is required to reach 1.5 degrees. Under business as usual, the world would warm by 2.7 degrees.[31]

So, government pledges aren't enough, and none of the short-term goals that governments have is being implemented fast enough.

While more regular citizens are prioritizing climate change, only half of US adults, for example, say dealing with climate change should be a top priority for the president and Congress.[32] It's difficult for governments to fix an issue that isn't a priority for their citizens. This is why, if you're concerned about climate change, being vocal about it to your political representatives is really important.

It's also still profitable for governments to keep financing fossil fuels, and for companies to keep polluting the environment. Couple this with the lack of urgency among the public, and governments can continue to move slowly without making the difficult choice to completely change the way the economy and society have been functioning for decades.

27   Who is truly responsible for climate change?

Playing the climate change blame game quickly becomes very tricky because it's not as easy as attributing emissions to each person to determine how at fault they are. Someone whose country doesn't support green infrastructure may emit more than someone else whose country does, but is that person therefore more to blame for climate change?

Fossil fuel companies are the first climate culprits that come to mind: a report released in 2017 found that just 100 fossil fuel companies were responsible for 70 per cent of global emissions for the past two decades.[33]

Of course, these fossil fuels are being used by corporations and private citizens and are subsidized by governments. But because fossil fuel companies have actively blocked measures that may replace them and be better for the planet, they can be seen as more culpable for the climate crisis than individuals.

The richest 1 per cent of people on the planet also emit nearly half of all emissions. To put this into perspective, if you are a household of one in the UK earning £30,000 a year (post-tax), then you're richer than 98 per cent of the world. Those who are more well off tend to consume more, fly more, eat more meat, and have bigger cars. While they aren't directly to blame for climate change, wealthier people do have the freedom to be more sustainable if they choose.

It's difficult to answer exactly who may be responsible for climate change because the capitalist, inherently unequal system we live in has allowed for the crisis to get to this stage. It's now down to those who have the power and passion to change the system to do so.

28   Why ecological empathy is important

The modern human lives a life far removed from the natural world. Most of us have moved away from rural areas to urban metropolises and only interact with nature in the form of green space, parks thinly scattered in between concrete and skyscrapers. But the modern human needs to relearn ecological empathy if the human species is to survive.

Ecological empathy is about having a connection with nature and feeling concern for non-human entities. Indigenous peoples have been living in a symbiotic way with Earth for millennia, and ecological empathy is an integral part of many Indigenous cultures.

As human societies have modernized, human connection with nature has depleted. This can be seen as the root of climate change because industrialized humans associate nature (plants, trees, natural gas) only with its utilitarian value – what they can get out of it – abandoning a sense of oneness with nature.

Even though Indigenous peoples have been living symbiotically with and protecting the Earth for generations, they are one of the groups suffering the most because of climate change.

Once we stop thinking of nature as something we can use, but something we depend on and are part of, then we can begin to repair our relationship with it. This is the power of ecological empathy.

29   What is climate optimism?

Learning and talking about climate change can be tough. Even though humanity has persisted through big problems such as global pandemics and the threat of nuclear war, the sheer scale of the damage already done to the planet and marginalized people can be enough to send anyone into a hopeless spiral of hopelessness.

Climate optimism is about making a concerted effort to stay hopeful, and to use hope as a power source in the fight to save the planet. Think about it: if you feel pessimistic, it can be difficult to motivate yourself to take any action at all. Optimism is a form of power.

Stopping climate change has so many benefits that go beyond just keeping the atmosphere cool. Through climate solutions and climate justice, we can make a better society that prioritizes human and animal happiness and health, not corporate profits. We can create systems that are equitable and give everyone a fair chance at life. We can all breathe clean, healthy air and look after our society's most vulnerable members. If we can pull it off, the upsides are huge.

30   The cost of fixing climate change – and the cost of not

Fixing climate change will be expensive. But the cost of not fixing it will be even greater – not just in terms of money but also in terms of human and animal lives.

If we act and fix it now, it's likely that living standards all over the world will be better than before in the form of reduced air pollution, lower household energy bills, more flexible transportation and higher-quality, healthier consumer goods.

It's estimated that, all in all, the cost of tackling the climate crisis will cost 1 per cent of global gross domestic product (GDP) every year until 2050.[34] To put this into perspective, we already spend 6 per cent of global GDP subsidizing fossil fuels.[35]

The cost of doing nothing will include billions in lost GDP, as well as rising seas and catastrophic flooding, widespread death and sickness related to extreme weather events, droughts, food and water shortages, increased energy costs, species extinction, habitat destruction, pollution and more pandemics. The longer we wait to tackle this crisis, the more expensive it will get.

References

1   Shaftel, H. (2022). What is the greenhouse effect? *NASA global climate change.*
    https://climate.nasa.gov/

2   Fecht, S. (2021). How exactly does carbon dioxide cause global warming? *Columbia Climate School*, 25 February.
    https://news.climate.columbia.edu/

3   IPCC (2007). *Climate change 2007: Synthesis report, contribution of Working Groups I, II and III to the Fourth Assessment Report of the Intergovernmental Panel on Climate Change*, ed. Pachauri, R. K., and Reisinger, A. IPCC.

4   Vallero, D. A. (2019). Air pollution biogeochemistry. In *Air pollution calculations* (pp. 175–206). Elsevier.

5   Friedlingstein, P. et al. (2020). Global carbon budget 2020. *Earth System Science Data, 12*: 3269–3340.

6   WWF and RSPB (2017). Understanding the UK's overseas footprint for deforestation-risk commodities. *Risky Business.*
    wwf.org.uk/riskybusiness

7   Lawson, S. (2014). *An analysis of the extent and nature of illegality in forest conversion for agriculture and timber plantations.* Forest Trends and Report Series: Consumer Goods and Deforestation, September. https://www.forest-trends.org/wp-content/uploads/imported/for168-consumer-goods-and-deforestation-letter-14-0916-hr-no-crops_web-pdf.pdf

8   FAO (2021). *Forest governance by indigenous and tribal peoples,* facts and figures. Food and Agriculture Organization. https://www.fao.org/3/cb2953en/online/src/html/copyright.html

9   Climate Watch, Historical GHG emissions, emissions by sector. www.climatewatchdata.org/

10 The Royal Society (2021). *The basics of climate change.* https://royalsociety.org/, 17 November.

11 CO2 Earth (2022). Latest daily CO2. www.co2.earth/. Last updated 3:35:02 AM on 4 February 2022, Hawaii local time (UTC -10).

12 Callendar, G. S. (1938). The artificial production of carbon dioxide and its influence on temperature. *Quarterly Journal of the Royal Meteorological Society, 64*(275): 223–240.

13 Hall, S. (2015). Exxon knew about climate change almost 40 years ago. *Scientific American,* 26 October.

14 Climate Action Tracker (2021). Temperatures. https://climateactiontracker.org/. Last updated 9 November 2021.

15 Friends of the Earth Scotland and Global Witness (2021). A review of the role of fossil fuel based carbon capture and storage in the energy system. *Report: Fossil Fuel Carbon Capture & Storage.*

16 Doyle, J. (2011). Where has all the oil gone? BP branding and the discursive elimination of climate change risk. In *Culture, environment and ecopolitics* (pp. 200–225). Essay, Cambridge Scholars.

17 Yoder, K. (2021, September 21). *Why do oil companies care so much about your carbon footprint?* Grist. Retrieved May 16, 2022, from https://grist.org/energy/footprint-fantasy/

18 Kaufman, M. (2021, July 9). *The devious fossil fuel propaganda we all use.* Mashable. Retrieved May 16, 2022, from https://mashable.com/feature/carbon-footprint-pr-campaign-sham

19 Ogilvy & Mather Chicago (2007). *BP Carbon Footprint Calculator.* New webby gallery + index. Retrieved May 16, 2022, from https://winners.webbyawards.com/2007/websites/general-websites/lifestyle/143421/bp-carbon-footprint-calculator

20 IEA (2021). *Global Energy Review: CO2 Emissions in 2020.* International Energy Agency. www.iea.org/

21 Oxfam (2020). Carbon emissions of richest 1 percent more than double the emissions of the poorest half of humanity. Oxfam, 21 September.

22 IPCC (2021). Climate change widespread, rapid, and intensifying. International Panel on Climate Change, 9 August.

23 Levin, K. (2018). Half a degree and a world apart: The difference in climate impacts between 1.5°C and 2°C of warming. World Resources Institute, 7 October.

24 Climate Action Tracker (2021). Countries. Last updated December 2021.

25 IPCC (2021). *Climate Change 2021: The Physical Science Basis. Sixth Assessment Report of the Intergovernmental Panel on Climate Change.* Cambridge University Press.

26 IEA (2021). *World Energy Investment 2021.* International Energy Agency. www.iea.org/reports/world-energy-investment-2021

27 Win, T. L. (2018). France is the world's most food sustainable country. *World Economic Forum*, 28 November.

28 Osman-Elasha, B. (2014). Women ... In the shadow of climate change. *UN Chronicle, 46*(4).

29 The World Bank (2020). Population growth (annual). https://data.worldbank.org/

30 REN21 (2021). *Renewables 2021, Global Status Report,* https://www.ren21.net

31 Climate Action Tracker (2021). Glasgow's 2030 credibility gap: Net zero's lip service to climate action, 9 November.

32 Funk, C., & Kennedy, B. (2020). How Americans see climate change and the environment in 7 charts, *Pew Research Center*, 21 April.

33 Griffin, P. (2017). *CDP Carbon Majors Report 2017*. The Carbon Majors Database, July.

34 Imperial College London (2020). *How will acting on climate change affect the economy?* Grantham Institute: Climate Change and the Environment, 20 March.

35 Coady, D., Parry, I., Nghia-Piotr, & Baoping, S. (2019). Global fossil fuel subsidies remain large: An update based on country-level estimates. Working Paper No. 19/89, 2 May.

CHAPTER 2

ENERGY

31   Energy holds the key

Energy is responsible for around 70 per cent of greenhouse gas emissions globally, which means solving the energy problem has the greatest potential for solving the climate challenge.[1]

Even though governments around the world have made pledges and held climate talks since the 1990s, emissions from energy have still increased by 60 per cent.

Since fossil fuels were first discovered, they've been used to create energy for modern humanity to develop and grow prosperous economies. We need energy to power almost everything that's relevant to modern life – our kitchen and bathroom appliances, heating for our homes, the trains we use to commute to work, our phones, our work Zoom calls.

But fossil fuel dependence has come at a dire cost to the planet and to vulnerable people. The good news is, we don't have to give up modern technology and regress to life before the Industrial Revolution to save the planet. We already have the technology to drive down emissions; we just need to move quickly, change policies and invest in clean energy.

32   How does saving energy save the planet?

Our entire global economy has been built with fossil fuels in mind, which means we rely on them to keep society going. Fossil fuels are burned to heat our homes, to give us electricity so we can watch TV, to power the trucks that stock our supermarkets, and to carry our garbage away.

Until these activities are powered with clean renewable energy, our energy usage directly correlates with damage to the planet. That's why, right now, saving energy will save fossil fuels from being burned, which will decrease the negative effect to the planet.

This doesn't mean we should all start living off the grid or extremely frugal lifestyles. It means we should save energy if we can, and simultaneously push our governments to invest in renewable energy quickly.

33   Where does our energy come from?

Most countries around the world rely on fossil fuels like coal, oil and natural gas to produce energy. Since around the 1940s, global energy usage has exploded and continues to rise exponentially. Compared to fossil fuels, renewables like solar and wind energy still make up a tiny percentage of the energy mix globally.

Fossil fuel power plants create energy by burning coal or oil, using the heat generated to create steam that drives turbines. Fossil fuels create electricity quite reliably and are not subject to changes in weather, as renewables sometimes are. We just decide to burn fossil fuels, and we have energy. But as reliable as they are, fossil fuels emit planet-warming greenhouse gases and toxic air pollution.

The biggest barriers to renewables being adopted so far have been cost, logistics and lack of political will.

Fortunately, in 2020, most renewables became cheaper than the cheapest fossil fuel.[2] So, hopefully, the prospect of saving money should encourage governments to make the switch.

34   How did the Industrial Revolution warm our planet?

The Industrial Revolution was a pivotal moment in human history, defined by the invention of machines that made products quickly and in huge quantities. Before these machines were introduced, products used to be made by hand, sometimes taking days or weeks to produce.

Industry's shift to machinery was accelerated by the invention of the steam engine, which burned coals to heat water whose steam powered the engine. Steam power was used to grow economies, mine for more fossil fuels, and run factories, railroads and ships, all of which emitted huge amounts of greenhouse gases into the atmosphere.

Warming resulting from these activities was first observed in the 1830s – not in the regions where the Industrial Revolution began but in tropical and Arctic regions.[3] Almost two centuries later, the warming effects of industrialization are clear all over the world.

Even though we have technological innovations that allow us to harness the incredible power of the Sun and the wind, we continue to use industrial technology that uses fossil energy, and simply because that's how it's always been done. It's time for a change, don't you think?

35   What are the different fossil fuels and how do they contribute to climate change?

The levels of greenhouse gases in the atmosphere are higher than they've been in three million years, all because of our society's dependence on million-year-old remains of plants and animals. Let's learn about the different types of fossil fuel.[4]

Coal is a solid rock and the most carbon-intensive fossil fuel, made from the energy of dead plants that were buried and pressurized under layers of dirt and rock over millions of years. Coal is the dirtiest fuel: it releases more carbon dioxide than oil or gas, and also emits mercury, arsenic and soot pollution. In 2020, coal held the second largest share of the energy mix, accounting for around 27 per cent of the world's energy usage.

Oil or petroleum is a liquid fossil fuel made from the bodies of marine animals and plants. Over time, sand and rock covered these remains, exerting heat and pressure which created what we now call petroleum. As of 2020, oil, at around 31 per cent, has the largest share of the energy mix.

Natural gas is made mostly of methane and is found in the holes of porous rocks, usually near deposits of petroleum. Natural gas is usually used for heating and cooking in homes, which releases greenhouse gas emissions. In 2020, natural gas consumption increased to a record high, making up around 25 per cent of the energy mix.

36   Why is it important to know about renewable energy?

In the upcoming years, there will be significant changes to how our energy system works, and it's important to be aware of the pros and cons between different types of renewable energy. Some types of renewable energy seem great on the surface but may have unforeseen disadvantages.

You may be responsible for voting in your country's next government, which will have the monumental task of curbing emissions to avert disaster. Being an informed citizen will help you vote in favour of the planet and your community. For the next few sections, we'll learn about the different types of renewable energy and their benefits and drawbacks.

37   The behemoths: solar and wind energy

Solar and wind energy are probably the best-known renewables, and for good reason. The amount of solar energy that could meet humanity's energy needs for a year hits the Earth in just the space of an hour, while wind is in high supply almost everywhere in the world. If we harness these sources of energy, we can have free, unlimited energy.

Until recently, the challenge with these types of energy has been their dependence on the weather. What do you do if the wind isn't blowing and the sun isn't shining? This is why upgrades in energy storage technology have been so key to moving this technology forward, and why investments in battery capacities have increased dramatically over the past few years.

Luckily, the price of solar and wind has been coming down enough to compete even with the cheapest fossil fuels, so it's now down to governments to make the switch quickly.

38 The power of water: hydropower and tidal energy

Water is one of the most powerful substances on Earth, strong enough that we can use its immense energy to spin turbines to create electricity. There are two types of energy that are produced using water: hydroelectricity and tidal.

Hydroelectricity is created by storing water in a dam until it's released, which is a clean and renewable way of creating energy.

However, dams can do some damage to natural river flow ecosystems and severely disrupt local wildlife. The hydropower industry has also been accused of having a murky human rights record, often displacing Indigenous riverside communities and disrupting the livelihood of those who depend on rivers.

Tidal power is similar to hydroelectricity, but it uses the energy of naturally occurring river and ocean tides. Think of tidal energy like wind energy underwater – turbines are placed in areas where tides pull the water in at high speeds, turning the turbines and creating electricity. Tidal energy is still in development, so only time will tell if it can become a reliable part of the energy mix.

It's important to be critical and understand the risks and benefits of energy sources. Earth's water systems are powerful, but we must be careful not to disrupt water ecosystems and Indigenous communities in the search for clean energy.

39 The Earth's core is as hot as the Sun, so why don't we use geothermal energy more?

Geothermal energy comes from heat inside the Earth, stored inside rocks and liquid water beneath the crust of the planet. To access this energy, wells are dug thousands of metres deep to reach underground reservoirs of steam and hot water.

Geothermal is a reliable source of renewable energy, and once a heat pump is set up, it requires very little maintenance. But there are some greenhouse gas emissions released during the process of digging to find reservoirs, although this process emits far fewer greenhouse gases than fossil fuels do.

Right now, we're harnessing only a very small percentage of geothermal energy potential. This is because geothermal energy is difficult to locate, and perfect spots to harness this energy are geographically quite limited. There are also huge upfront costs associated with drilling down deep into the Earth.

40   Is there really plant power in biofuels?

A biofuel is a fuel made from plants – even burning wood to generate fire counts as a biofuel.

Biofuels are renewable sources of energy, and any carbon released during burning is compensated by the carbon absorbed as the plant grew. This makes the energy carbon neutral, unlike other renewables, which eventually become carbon negative.

Bioethanol and biodiesel are the main types of biofuel and can be made either from fermenting corn or sugar or using vegetable oils. Biodiesel can be used in diesel cars right now, and they have the benefit of being biodegradable and non-toxic.

However, there's a major catch: to produce all that plant matter to turn into fuel, we need a lot of farmland. Farmers would have to be incentivized to start growing biofuel crops rather than food, so there would be a real chance that producing biofuels on a big scale could affect food supply or even drive up food prices.

Biofuels that are grown using land that could be used to grow food are called first-generation fuels, and big oil companies have been advertising (read: greenwashing) these for years.

Second-generation fuels are a better option: these are fuel crops grown on land where edible food can't be grown. But these are unlikely to become price competitive anytime soon because this type of land is quite limited and difficult to grow on.

41 Nuclear power: friend or foe?

Many governments around the world have included nuclear energy in their plans for a green transition. But is that a good idea?

First, a little science: nuclear energy comes from the process of splitting atoms of the element uranium, which creates heat. This heats up water, producing steam that turns turbines and creates electricity.

Nuclear energy doesn't release any greenhouse gases like coal and petrol do, so technically it's a sustainable energy source and doesn't contribute to climate change.

So why is it controversial? Nuclear energy has long been contentious in the energy industry because of the waste it produces and the dangerous nature of handling radioactive materials. If the uranium is handled improperly, or radioactive waste is accidentally released, people living near nuclear plants are at huge risk. Disposing of nuclear waste is also a challenge – it takes hundreds of thousands of years to deactivate the spent fuel.

Nuclear power is not a renewable resource. There are 80 years' worth of fuel in known uranium reserves if used at current rates. There are ways to extract uranium from seawater, however, which could make nuclear energy completely renewable, but the science on that is still imperfect.

Despite its downsides, switching to nuclear power is being considered as a way to quickly transition to net zero and meet the world's energy needs until the capacity of other clean energy sources increases. Nuclear power plants operate at a very high capacity and have a small land footprint.

It's up to us to decide – if nuclear energy is necessary to avoid climate catastrophe and to encourage a faster transition to renewables, then maybe the risks are worth it.

42 The outlook for renewables – what does the future look like?

One thing is for certain: if we want to be able to live on this planet, we need most of our energy to come from renewables quickly.

Solar and wind energy are expected to grow the fastest in the 2020s, due to their plummeting cost and higher reliability as opposed to other renewables. Other renewables such as hydroelectric and geothermal energy are expected to grow as well. Some studies estimate that the entire world could be completely powered by renewables by 2050. This would save 4–7 million lives annually from air pollution worldwide.[5] But there are still major technological hurdles – around half of the reductions in emissions by 2050 will come from technologies that are still at the prototype phase.[6]

In the future, most cars on the roads will be electric, and planes will be relying on biofuels or other synthetic fuels that emit fewer greenhouse gas emissions. Factories and industrial plants will also probably be using carbon-capture technologies.

We know that the majority of greenhouse gas emissions on the planet come from burning fossil fuels for energy. If we can use the Sun's energy or wind energy to keep fossil fuels unburned and in the ground, that's a huge win for the planet and for us.

Thanks to reductions in the cost of renewables and improving technologies, governments will definitely be encouraged to make the switch faster – if not for the planet, then at least for their pockets.

43   What's that word ... fracking?

Fracking is a word that dominated headlines for many years in the United States, especially when President Trump repealed President Obama's policies for setting environmental standards on the practice. But what is it and why is it controversial?

Fracking is short for 'hydraulic fracturing', which is the process that injects 'fracking liquid' into rock to crack it open and access fossil fuel deposits.

The controversy around this practice arises because the fracking liquid used in the process can potentially contaminate drinking water by leaking into groundwater. The wastewater produced from fracking can also accidentally leak from landfills, during transportation, or when equipment fails. This can endanger local communities near to where fracking takes place. Even more worryingly, a massive amount of water is needed to create fracking liquid, so water supplies can become severely stressed as a result, especially in areas where water is scarce.

Governments are starting to realize that fracking is not compatible with a safe and healthy future for people and the planet. Plenty of countries have strict regulations on fracking, and the practice itself is expensive. Hopefully, we'll be seeing the last of 'fracking' very soon.

44   Why can't we switch to renewables right now?

The cost of renewable energy has plummeted over the past few years, so wouldn't it make sense to switch over right now?

It would be nice if we could immediately switch to clean energy, but there are huge obstacles like limitations of supply and existing infrastructure which are slowing things down. Renewables tend to rely on natural weather phenomena like wind, water and sunshine. But these sources of energy can be unreliable and inconsistent, and the technology developed to store this energy isn't perfect yet.

Our existing energy system is also a barrier to moving to 100 per cent renewable because it's often cheaper for energy suppliers to continue using fossil fuels rather than building new infrastructure that supports renewables.

But with the right amount of political will, these obstacles are not impossible to overcome.

The governments of high-income countries need to start directly investing in clean energy research and technology, as well as stopping subsidies for fossil fuels. This is where voters can have some control, by electing leaders who make this a priority.

45   Fossil fuel companies have known about climate change for decades ...

... and they have protected their profits instead. Fossil fuel and coal companies have known since 1966 that their actions would cause climate change.[7] They've lobbied and argued against carbon dioxide regulation since the 1980s.[8] They have tried to discredit scientists who studied the effects of carbon emissions on the planet.[9] They run PR campaigns that shift the responsibility of climate change onto the individual rather than themselves.

It's painful to think we had a chance to stop this current crisis decades ago but were thwarted by people who were more motivated by the prospect of making money. This book empowers you to take action as an individual in your community, but we must remind ourselves who is responsible for the crisis we're in.

Unfortunately, we can't go back in time and stop these companies from committing crimes against our planet, but we can band together and help to clean up the mess they've made. And we can do that by staying optimistic and fighting for justice for those who will suffer the harshest consequences.

46   Why is coal so dirty?

Whatever you might have heard about coal, it's probably not been great. The phrase 'coal mine' evokes claustrophobic images of exploited men cramped into a small space, risking their lives and breathing in toxic fumes.

In the 1900s in the United States, it wasn't uncommon for prisons to send Black men to work in coal mines as part of their punishment. Coal mining is an exceptionally dangerous job – caves can collapse on workers, explosions can occur, and temperatures can be scorching hot.

Aside from being dirty ethically, the process of using coal for energy heavily pollutes the air and surrounding ecosystems.

Coal combustion releases sulphur dioxide and nitrogen oxide which can cause acid rain, as well as other toxic chemicals and heavy metals which can contaminate drinking water. It also releases smog and tiny particles of ash that are damaging to our lungs.

Some studies have also found that this ash carries more radiation into the environment than a nuclear power plant.[10]

Coal is far too dirty on all fronts, so we need to stop mining and using it – for the sake of people and planet.

47   Simple ways to reduce how much energy you use

The most important action we can take as citizens to reduce emissions from energy is to push our governments to make the switch to renewables to power the energy grid. In the meantime, you can reduce emissions from energy by using less of it.

Here are some simple actions you can take to cut down on your own energy usage, with more detailed explanations of each action to come in upcoming sections:

- Insulate your home well.
- Get a smart thermometer for your home.
- Upgrade to energy-efficient appliances.
- Take trains instead of planes.
- Eat more plants and less meat.
- Buy second-hand.

48 How climate change can make our energy needs worse

When I first moved to London, I remember a day in July when temperatures reached over 40 degrees Celsius. This kind of extreme heat used to be exceptionally rare for a place with usually mild summer weather, but it's going to become ever more frequent. And in places where summers are already hot, the temperature could become unbearable.

A paper published in *Nature Communications* in 2019 found that future energy demand is going to increase by as much as 25 per cent even under moderate global warming.[11]

When summers are hotter and longer, people use air conditioning and cooling systems more, which drives up energy demand and could make climate change even worse.

Demand for energy is going to increase, and we need to meet this demand using renewable energy to stop this dangerous feedback loop.

49 The energy that goes towards food waste

Every item of food you eat represents the energy and natural resources that went into growing and creating it.

We use land and water to grow crops and energy to power the tractors that harvest the crops, the factories that process the raw materials, and the trucks that transport the food to supermarkets. Any amount of food wasted represents wasted energy and resources that could have been saved or diverted to something else.

Food is wasted at every level of production: in high-income countries, a higher proportion of food is wasted at the consumer level, while in low-income countries, food is usually wasted before it reaches consumers.[12] Global food waste alone accounts for almost 10 per cent of greenhouse gas emissions.[13]

Food waste is energy waste. But there are some projects being worked on that could convert food waste into energy by using anaerobic digestion to create biogas.[14] This is when organic waste breaks down in an oxygen-free environment and produces gas made of methane and carbon dioxide that can be used to replace fossil fuels for energy.

50   The energy challenge in emerging economies

Developing and emerging countries hold two-thirds of the world's population but account for only one-fifth of investment in clean energy.[15]

Emerging economies are growing, which means the demand for energy in these countries is going to increase. It's going to be a considerable challenge to be able to meet the demand for this energy and improve quality of life without making climate change worse.

To make matters more difficult, the COVID-19 pandemic has meant that the money that these countries had set aside for clean energy has been reallocated, which has been disrupting any chances of a green recovery.

Emerging economies will need to increase their investment in clean energy from $150 billion in 2020 to over $1 trillion in 2030. But this is not an impossible task. Because energy infrastructure in emerging economies is being built from scratch, it's easier and cheaper to build clean energy systems from the get-go, rather than retrofitting old technology, which is what developed countries will need to do.

For perspective, emerging economies could save up to $165 billion over the lifetime of renewable energy added in 2020 alone.

Cost will be a huge factor in determining whether emerging economies choose to use renewable energy. The outlook is pretty good – the next chapter will tell us why.

51   Is dirty energy cheaper than clean energy?

When I was born in 1996, the price of oil was around $30 per barrel (adjusting for inflation).[16] As I write this, a barrel is around $90, and it's only getting more expensive.[17]

Solar power is now the cheapest energy source in history, cheaper than coal and gas in most countries. In 2020, for the first time, it's cheaper to power the economy with renewable energy than with fossil fuels. No longer can oil company apologists claim that being green doesn't make economic sense.

So no, dirty energy is not cheaper than clean energy. And we'd be smart to switch to clean energy fast.

52   How do fossil fuels impact Indigenous peoples?

For almost seven years, Indigenous organizations, primarily led by women, protested to stop construction of Canadian oil company Enbridge's new pipeline from Alberta, Canada, to Lake Superior in Minnesota.[18] In October 2021, the line became operational regardless, ignoring Indigenous peoples' sovereignty and their right to a healthy environment. The possibility of a spill means the pipeline threatens the health of crops and farmland, as well as non-human animals in the area.

Indigenous peoples' rights have long been disregarded by many fossil fuel companies, which have been invading territories to perform extractions for decades. Even so, Indigenous peoples' brave resistance to pipelines saved almost a billion tonnes of carbon dioxide per year over the 2010s, by stopping or delaying construction of new projects.[19]

Governments will need to be mindful to respect Indigenous sovereignty when investing in renewable energy. We'll talk more about this later in this chapter.

53   What is energy inequality?

The average person living in the UK produces more carbon dioxide emissions in two days than the average person in the Democratic Republic of Congo produces in a whole year.

Fundamental differences in energy infrastructure mean that people in developing countries have access to less energy, which contributes to a continuous cycle of poverty and inequality.

Rich countries pledged in 2021 to stop funding international fossil fuel projects but will still be going ahead with domestic energy projects. This could make energy inequality worse because developing countries may not have the funding to support their energy needs at all, let alone switch over to renewables.

Countries in the Global South will be left to deal with the consequences of climate change brought on by the consumption of those in the Global North, and, to add insult to injury, will be unable to meet the energy needs of their citizens. This is energy inequality, and richer countries need to take responsibility for their part in creating this injustice.

54   Let go of consumerism to save energy

The number-one way to reduce the amount of energy we use is simply to buy less stuff. We live in a consumerist culture that psychologically manipulates us into thinking we need to buy things to feel included, accepted or worthy. The global economic system grows and thrives if more stuff is made and more stuff is bought, even if the planet and other people suffer as a result. And indeed, today we're buying way more things we don't need than ever before.

Overconsumption has a huge impact on the environment, especially when we buy things we don't need, because every single product we buy is made using natural resources and fossil fuels. Social media and celebrity culture all contribute to the idea that we need to buy if we are to 'keep up'. Influencers peddle a different fast-fashion product every week; people on TikTok show off their sleek kitchens and usher us to their Amazon links, and people's insecurities are targeted by Photoshopped ads on Instagram selling skincare 'solutions'.

The lavish lifestyles of the ultra-rich also set the tone for what the rest of society should aspire to, driving home even further the idea that your worth can be measured by how much you consume.

We have the power to reject these messages that make us feel we need to buy things we don't need in order to feel worthy, and thereby save resources.

55 Let's talk about energy sovereignty

Bernardo Caal Xol is a teacher and community leader of the Maya Q'eqchi' Indigenous community in north central Guatemala, sentenced to seven years' imprisonment for protesting against a hydroelectric project.

The hydropower plants in question have been constructed on the Cahabón River, which is not only sacred to the Q'eqchi' people but relied upon for food and water. By going ahead with the construction and jailing Bernardo, the government and the company behind the project have violated human rights and ignored the energy sovereignty of the Q'eqchi' people.

Energy sovereignty is the idea that everyone, especially Indigenous communities, deserves the right to make their own decisions about energy systems. Indigenous peoples around the world are often victims of energy colonialism, which is when a foreign party invades historic and cultural land for the purpose of producing energy for themselves. In this context, the term 'foreign party' means any non-Indigenous entity. Indigenous communities are not only exposed to the negative effects of an energy project, but also silenced, punished, and sometimes murdered for protesting.

Energy sovereignty gives power back to these communities and allows them to decide for themselves whether they would like an oil pipeline or a wind power project in their neighbourhood. It also means respecting their wishes if they choose not to host these projects.

56   How renewable energy can violate the rights of Indigenous peoples

Indigenous peoples are one of the groups most vulnerable to the effects of climate change, but they are also one of the most powerful agents of change. Indigenous culture and tradition usually place great importance on having a close relationship with nature, which means many Indigenous peoples are at the forefront of advocating for a just transition to a green economy. This is not the only reason why governments need to involve Indigenous peoples in climate decision making, however: *not* involving them can violate their rights.

Historically, colonization in the Americas has displaced many Indigenous peoples from fertile land to land that was once considered undesirable or unprofitable but which is now sought after by renewable energy companies. Solar power works well in arid areas, wind power works well in hilly areas, and hydropower works well in steep areas, all of which are places Indigenous peoples were exiled to.

Governments often grant permits to renewable energy companies to start building in these areas, ignoring the land rights of Indigenous peoples.

We can't allow the transition to a green economy to infringe on the rights of Indigenous peoples. This is just another example of why taking climate justice into account is so important when thinking about solutions for saving the planet.

57　What is Earth Overshoot Day?

Earth Overshoot Day is the day of the year when humanity has exhausted nature's supply of natural resources that can be sustainably regenerated in a year.[20] In 2021, Earth Overshoot Day fell on 29 July. This means that anything consumed after this date up to the end of the year is a debt to the planet and to future generations.

Generally speaking, higher-income countries like those in the Global North consume much more than lower-income countries, which means Overshoot Day isn't the same everywhere.

For example, Qatar's Overshoot Day is 9 February. If everyone lived like the average person in Qatar, we would need nine Earths! The United States' and Canada's Overshoot Day is 14 March, and most European countries use up Earth's resources before the end of May.

Some countries, like India, don't even have an Overshoot Day. These countries contribute the least to climate change but will often bear the consequences of the climate crisis. This is called climate injustice.

58　Does buying second-hand save energy?

Absolutely. If you buy a piece of furniture second-hand, you save resources and energy that would have been used to create a new piece of furniture, and you save the furniture from going to landfill. The same goes for cars, clothing, toys, appliances – pretty much anything you can physically buy.

There are benefits to buying second-hand that go beyond the environment, too. You can save money and buy high-quality products that last a long time for a cheaper price, you can acquire unique items, and you can send a message to mass producers that their unethical practices won't fly.

59　Does buying local save energy?

It's never been easier to buy products made from all around the world but buying locally is a better way to save energy and contribute to your local community. By supporting local businesses, you can have a direct positive effect on the health of your community, because local businesses tend to employ local people and have ethical practices.

However, it's important to think critically as a consumer because some local businesses need parts shipped in from elsewhere, which might not make your purchase environmentally friendly after all.

Like anything in sustainability, weighing up multiple factors is the best way to make a responsible purchase decision. If you want to learn about the environmental effect of buying local food specifically, head to Chapter 4: Food.

References

1   IEA (2021). *Net Zero by 2050: A roadmap for the global energy sector.* International Energy Agency, October.

2   IRENA (2021). *Renewable power generation costs in 2020.* International Renewable Energy Agency.

3   Abram, N., McGregor, H., Tierney, J. et al. (2016). Early onset of industrial-era warming across the oceans and continents. *Nature, 536*: 411–418. https://doi.org/10.1038/nature19082

4   BP (2021). *Statistical review of world energy.* British Petroleum, July.

5   WHO (2021). *Household air pollution and health.* World Health Organization, 22 September.

6   IEA (2021). *Net zero by 2050: A roadmap for the global energy sector.* International Energy Agency, October.

7   Young, E. (2019). Coal knew, too. *Huffington Post,* last updated 16 December 2019.

8   Thacker, P. D. (2021). The dirty dozen documents of Big Oil's secret climate knowledge. *DeSmog,* 2 November.

9   Climate Reality Project (2019). The climate denial machine: How the fossil fuel industry blocks climate action. Climate Reality Project, 5 September.

10 Zakaria, N., Ba'an, R., & Kathiravale, S. (2010). Radiological impact from airborne routine discharges of coal-fired power plant. Malaysian Nuclear Agency, 26–28 October.

11 Van Ruijven, B. J., De Cian, D., & Ian Wing, S. (2019). Amplification of future energy demand growth due to climate change. *Nature Communications, 10*(2762). https://doi.org/10.1038/s41467-019-10399-3

12 FAO (2011). *Global food losses and food waste: Extent, causes and prevention.* Food and Agriculture Organization.

13 UNEP (2021). *Food Waste Index Report 2021.* United Nations Environment Programme, 4 March.

14 Paritosh, K., Kushwaha, S. K., Yadav, M., Pareek, N., Chawade, A., and Vivekanand, V. (2017). Food waste to energy: An overview of sustainable approaches for food waste management and nutrient recycling. *BioMed Research International*, Article ID 2370927. https://doi.org/10.1155/2017/237092

15 IEA (2021). Financing clean energy transitions in emerging and developing economies. International Energy Agency. https://www.iea.org/reports/financing-clean-energy-transitions-in-emerging-and-developing-economies

16 McMahon, T. (2021). Historical crude oil prices, inflation data. https://inflationdata.com, 13 October.

17 Fanzeres, J., & Tobben, S. (2022). WTI crude passes $90 a barrel for the first time since 2014. *Bloomberg Markets*, 2 February.

18 Lake, O. O., & Quaid, K. (2021). Indigenous women lead the movement to stop Line 3 pipeline: This is everything we have. *Ms. Magazine*, 24 May.

19 Indigenous Environmental Network (2021). Indigenous resistance against carbon. August. https://www.ienearth.org/

20 Earth Overshoot Day (2021). Country Overshoot Days. https://www.overshootday.org

CHAPTER 3

OCEANS

60   The biggest sources of ocean plastic pollution

Try to wrap your head around this: one garbage truck of plastic enters our ocean every minute.[1] Plastic debris has been found everywhere – from the water's surface to the deepest depths of the sea, and it's only accumulating and increasing as the days go by.

Around 80 per cent of plastic pollution in the ocean originates from land.[2] Rain washes away plastic litter and debris from urban areas into rivers, lakes and streams, which all lead to the ocean.

The sizes of the different pieces range from large plastic bags to microscopic tyre particles that are sloughed off due to friction with the road. The rest of plastic pollution comes from fishing nets, discarded ropes and other human sources like cruise ships.

61   Can aquariums play a role in ocean conservation?

In a perfect world, aquariums that hold wild animals captive would not exist. Human entertainment is an ethically abhorrent reason to take animals away from their native homes.

Unfortunately, we don't live in a perfect world. The climate crisis is ravaging biodiversity in the ocean, and many species are on the brink of extinction.

Aquariums are playing an important role in marine conservation. For example, four of six fish species that are extinct in the wild are held in aquariums.[3] Some aquariums also regularly rescue and rehabilitate injured animals and contribute to scientific knowledge of how climate change is affecting marine animals.

Globally, we have failed to protect wild ecosystems from habitat loss, pollution, ocean acidification and exploitation. Although it's not ideal that we're now forced to protect species in captivity, there is no doubt that some aquariums are contributing positively to conservation and even increasing public awareness about climate change and protecting marine animals.

This should go without saying, but if you're interested in visiting an aquarium, do your research beforehand. Make sure that the animals are not used for entertainment and that the aquarium has a net positive effect on sea animals.

62   Most plastic pollution comes from a few of the world's rivers

The term 'riverine plastic emissions' describes plastic pollution that has entered the ocean via rivers. New research has uncovered that over 1,000 rivers account for 80 per cent of global riverine plastic emissions.[4] The top ten largest emitting rivers are all in Asia – seven in the Philippines, two in India and one in Malaysia.

In countries where infrastructure for waste management is poor, it can be all too easy for plastic waste to enter rivers. These countries also often experience frequent heavy rainfall, which can wash plastic into waterways.

Plastic pollution that enters the oceans affects the entire world, and richer countries have a responsibility to support lower-income countries to upgrade infrastructure and improve the way they manage plastic pollution. This is especially important because lower-income countries are often poor due to colonization (both past and present) by richer countries.

63   Why are sea levels rising and why is it bad?

Human civilizations have usually thrived around bodies of water – mainly coastlines, lakes and large rivers. Think of any major city around the world, and you'll probably find that it's near a body of water. Water is an incredible resource and has been used as a system of global trade and transportation for thousands of years.

That's why rising sea levels are such a cause for concern. If large human populations live near water, there could be widespread destruction and displacement if that water starts encroaching on land and swallowing up parts of or even entire cities.

Not only are floods more common than before (which can sometimes turn deadly), but essential infrastructure like roads, bridges and power lines could become severely disrupted if flooding occurs frequently.

Sea levels have risen some 21–24 centimetres (8–9½ in) since 1880.[5] Sea levels rise because of melting glaciers and ice sheets in the planet's polar regions, and also because ocean water tends to expand as it heats up.

In the Pacific Ocean, sea levels have been rising more rapidly than anywhere else.[6] Island nations in the Pacific could face the prospect of their countries becoming uninhabitable, even though they contribute very little to carbon emissions.

64   Ancient glacier bacteria – a cause for concern?

Scientists studying glacier ice have found ancient bacteria and viruses locked up in glaciers, frozen for thousands of years. These glaciers are like historic time capsules of ancient organisms – they teach us about the history of life on Earth and contribute to our understanding of microscopic life today.

Since glacier ice is melting at an unprecedented speed, scientists are losing precious time to study these organisms. As the ice melts, these organisms are also being released into seawater. Some viruses can remain active after being frozen for a long time, and some can't. It remains to be seen how the released organisms will affect our health, and scientists around the world have said it may be impossible to predict what will happen.

While this is not something you or I should worry about too much, it only reinforces how important it is for humans to stop warming the planet, and how there could be unexpected consequences.

65   How are oceans being acidified?

In the past 200 years, the ocean has become 30 per cent more acidic.[7] This is around ten times faster than any acidification in the past 55 million years. When there is more carbon dioxide in the atmosphere, more of it gets dissolved in seawater, which forms carbonic acid.[8] Carbonic acid makes seawater more acidic, which affects every single organism living in the ocean.

Life in the ocean has adapted to live in water with a certain acidity, or pH value (potential of hydrogen – or concentration of hydrogen ions) and may not be able to adapt fast enough to adjust to more acidic waters.

Governments must listen to scientists and commit to decreasing carbon dioxide emissions so the ocean's acidification can begin to stabilize.

66   Can we eat fish responsibly?

Seafood is delicious, has incredible health benefits, and is a staple food in many cultures around the world.

But rampant overfishing, widespread microplastics, food chain disruption and declining ocean health are decimating fish populations. Around 10 per cent of the global population (mostly people in the Global South) relies on fishing for their livelihood.[9] Fewer fish in the sea means fewer people fed.

The fish that are in low supply are those that are eaten the most in your country, so you should avoid eating those if you want to help the situation.

If you want to see an exhaustive list, I'd recommend checking out the UK's Marine Conservation Society which has a handy 'Good Fish Guide' on their website (www.mcsuk.org/goodfishguide/), where you can input your location and see which fish in your area are responsibly farmed.

A great rule of thumb to keep in mind: if you already eat fish a few times a week, try to reduce your consumption if you can.

67   The most endangered creatures in the sea

Some of the most beautiful and important creatures that live in the ocean are endangered because of human activity. Every single animal alive today has undergone a complex process of evolution over millions of years, but because of pollution and climate change, these animals are disappearing at an alarming rate.

- The vaquita porpoise is the most endangered cetacean in the world. The vaquita reproduces only once every two years and is found solely in the Gulf of California in Mexico. They die in fishing nets and from chlorinated pesticides that leak into the ocean.

- The hawksbill sea turtle is the smallest and most endangered sea turtle. They're hunted for their magnificent shells, which are used as decoration or jewellery.

- There are only a few thousand Florida manatees, also known as sea cows, left in the ocean. They are endangered because they routinely collide with boats or get tangled in fishing nets, and because their habitats have become polluted.

There are many more endangered animals on the Red List of Threatened Species (www.iucnredlist.org), which I encourage you to learn about.[10] Every single marine species is valuable and important, and losing even one is a tragedy.

These animals can't advocate for themselves, but you and I can advocate for them by telling everyone we know, reducing our fish intake, and supporting organizations that directly help these animals.

68   The countries polluting the ocean the most

Plastic pollution accidentally or deliberately ending up in the oceans is a huge issue for marine life. Once plastic enters the ocean, it's near-impossible to clean up. Countries that have poor waste management infrastructure tend to pollute the ocean with more plastic than others.

The ten countries that contribute the most plastic waste to the ocean are, in descending order: India, China, Indonesia, Brazil, Thailand, Mexico, Egypt, the United States, Japan and the UK.[11]

It's also worth noting that the United States, the UK and European countries are known for shipping their plastic waste to other countries – often countries with poor waste management.

Rich countries like the United States, South Korea and Australia also produce the highest amount of single-use plastic per person.

69   The companies polluting the ocean the most

Consumers are more aware than ever of climate change and are increasingly holding brands accountable on their green promises.

It can be easy to fall for well-polished greenwashing campaigns, but knowledge and awareness are the best tools against corporate spin. So let's have a look at some of the worst polluters in the corporate world.

The Break Free From Plastic Movement conducted a plastic waste audit and found that the Coca-Cola Company, PepsiCo, Unilever, Nestlé, Procter & Gamble, Mondelēz International, Philip Morris International, Danone, Mars, Inc., and Colgate-Palmolive made up the largest portion of plastic pollution in 2020.[12]

Oil spills are another form of ocean pollution, spelling disaster for marine life, clogging the blowholes of dolphins and whales and contributing to reproductive and digestive issues for thousands of species.

British Petroleum, or BP, was responsible for one of the worst oil spills in history, which happened in 2018 in the Gulf of Mexico. Thankfully, oil spills have become much less frequent this century – there are 90 per cent fewer spills today than in the 1970s.[13]

70   Which everyday products are harming the ocean?

The easiest way to make a positive impact to the ocean as an individual is to use ocean-friendly products in your daily life.

Microplastics, in particular, are impossible to clean once they're in the ocean. One of the biggest culprits of producing microplastics is when washing plastic clothing. They're also sometimes found in face washes and body scrubs as micro beads.

If you garden, switch to natural pesticides to protect the ocean from toxic runoff. If you smoke cigarettes, either quit or dispose of your cigarettes responsibly. Try to avoid single-use plastic wherever possible, including plastic straws, plastic bags and plastic cutlery.

71   How to explore the ocean responsibly

Seeing the ocean in person is a great way to enrich your appreciation for its downright beauty, wonder and mystery. The ocean is useful, yes. It provides us with water and food and oxygen. But it's also a marvel to behold, and exploring it can increase our appreciation for its simple existence, as opposed to how 'useful' it is.

If you'd like to explore the ocean by boat, make sure to skip the cruise ship and choose an electric boat. Electric boats are quiet, so they don't disrupt marine life, and they emit fewer carbon emissions.

Snorkelling is also an option if you want to explore underwater but do so with extreme caution. Sea animals and plants are extremely sensitive – do not touch any animals or corals and stay as far away as possible to avoid disturbing or damaging any ecosystems.

Deepening your connection to the ocean in a mindful, responsible way can help you become a more empathetic advocate for the oceans and all that live in them and depend on them.

72 Do beach clean-ups help?

There's nothing that ruins a beach trip more than seeing a plastic bag floating around in the water.

Plastic has been extraordinarily useful for humans. It's provided us with durable medical devices, convenient packaging and electronic appliances. But it's as useful to us as it is devastating to animals – especially those that live in the sea.

The only sure-fire way to make sure plastic bags stay out of the ocean for good is for humans to stop producing them in the first place. But until we move on to something else to replace plastic, beach clean-ups can undo some of the damage already done.

Every piece of plastic litter picked up in a beach clean-up is one fewer piece of plastic litter in the ocean which could poison or suffocate aquatic wildlife. Beach clean-ups are especially great because they have the advantage of scale. Lots of people picking up litter means lots of litter getting saved from going into the ocean.

Beach clean-ups are also necessary because every piece of garbage on the beach is pretty much guaranteed to make it into the ocean due to the changing tides and strengths of the waves.

So, yes: beach clean-ups make a huge difference!

73   Avoid buying souvenirs made from ocean materials

When you leave a place, especially an oceanside place, try to take nothing with you but memories. Souvenirs are often wasteful, and ones made from ocean materials like shells and coral are harmful.

The ocean's ecosystem has worked one way for millions of years – recycling dead matter from shells to create nutrients for other organisms. But the ocean souvenir business takes empty shells and bits of coral to resell as mementos for visitors. Not only does this disrupt the ecosystem, but some harvesting methods cause damage to reefs by raking the ocean floor.

Even dead shells serve a purpose in the ocean, functioning as shelter for small animals, providing a surface for algae to grow, and adding nutrients to the ecosystem as they break down.

We can all find ways to remember our trips without contributing to damaging the ocean ecosystem.

74   Does buying 'repurposed ocean plastic' help?

The recycled clothing market has only just started taking off, and it has the potential to play a huge role in the future of fashion.

Shoes, bags, and clothing can be made using recycled ocean plastic yarns. Discarded fishing nets can be made into pellets, ready to be moulded into different products like sunglasses or jewellery.

Ocean plastic repurposing programmes often use ocean-bound plastic, which is a term that describes plastic that was on its way to the ocean but hadn't made it yet. Plastic waste is usually mismanaged, which means it's likely to make its way into the ocean at some point.

Plastic is made from fossil fuels, so buying recycled plastic can decrease demand for fossil fuels. Buying products made from ocean plastic will also increase demand for recycled products, which could encourage other businesses to recycle plastic for their own products.

But there's a problem. Let's use an analogy to understand it. Say you're filling up a bath with the water on full strength and at the same time scooping out water with a mug. The water coming out of the tap is the amount of plastic we produce, and the mug is the amount of plastic we're recycling through various initiatives. But instead of turning off the tap, plastic production is set to increase by 40 per cent by 2030.[14]

Repurposing ocean plastic does help. But it doesn't solve the root of the problem. We need to reduce the amount of plastic we use before the problem becomes unsolvable.

75   What is coral bleaching?

As horrible as the word 'bleaching' sounds, coral bleaching is an apt description of the colour change that happens when algae living within corals leave the coral's tissue because of stress.[15]

Corals and algae depend on each other for survival. The algae supply the coral with food and oxygen and help to remove waste. The coral provides the algae with a safe surface and nutrients like carbon dioxide necessary for photosynthesis. When corals are stressed because of increased water temperature or acidification, they expel the algae from their tissues and lose their colour, becoming 'bleached'.

Corals can recover from bleaching, but only in a certain window of time if temperatures go back to normal. Otherwise, they are at risk of starvation.

To protect corals, we must stop burning fossil fuels and filling our atmosphere and oceans with carbon dioxide. As individuals, we can also do our bit to wear reef-safe sunscreen and support businesses and non-profit organizations that help conserve the reef.

76   The ocean is our biggest carbon sink

A carbon sink is something that removes carbon compounds from the atmosphere by accumulating and storing it either in soil or in vegetation. The ocean is the biggest carbon sink on Earth, absorbing as much as 25 per cent of carbon in our atmosphere.[16]

Carbon is dissolved in ocean water, which is then used by phytoplankton to produce organic matter, and this organic matter sinks to the bottom of the ocean where the carbon is locked up for sometimes hundreds of years.

Mangroves, seagrass beds and salt marshes also help the ocean soak up carbon. These marine plants store considerably more carbon than forests on land.[17]

77   How to connect with the ocean

Our modern lives are so far removed from the natural world that it might even seem absurd to try to connect with nature. In a capitalist system, we're taught that nature is to be used and exploited, not appreciated and nurtured. Many Indigenous peoples and coastal communities, by contrast, have a deep connection to, and knowledge of, the ocean and nature. This can improve your sense of belonging and happiness and even give you a sense of peace and serenity.

You can connect with the ocean by being mindful and present when you're observing it:

- Listen to the waves and let yourself be lulled by the rhythmic crashing.
- Look out to the horizon and consider how many millions of species call the ocean home.
- Consider that the ocean is the birthplace of all life – including yours.
- Thank the ocean for all it provides you.
- Finally, acknowledge the important role you can play in preserving the beauty of the ocean for future generations to enjoy.

78   The ocean is where plastic enters the food chain

When plastic is tossed or finds its way into the ocean, it's extremely difficult to track or clean up. Over time, the plastic breaks down into smaller pieces called micro plastics, which can easily be swallowed by small fish or birds. Sometimes algae grows on small pieces of plastic, which, to fish can make them look like a tasty treat.

This plastic accumulates in the fat and tissue of the animals.[18] If these animals are eaten, the plastic travels through the food chain and could end up being consumed by humans.

Scientists are not yet sure of the health impacts of plastic currently in the food chain. We do know that shellfish and crustaceans have the highest levels of microplastics among seafood.[19]

79   Our plastic clothing obsession is hurting the ocean

Almost 60 per cent of our clothing is made with polyester, a synthetic plastic made from petroleum.[20] Yes – the stuff we use to power our cars is also the stuff we wear on our bodies. Polyester is cheap and versatile, and it's everywhere in fashion.

Without polyester, fast-fashion companies probably wouldn't exist because clothing wouldn't be very cheap to make. For millennia, humans have used plant materials (hemp, linen, cotton) to make clothing, and these take time to grow, harvest and make into yarn. Cheap clothing has encouraged overconsumption, and the consequences for the environment are staggering. Not only does our cheap clothing often end up in landfill, but thousands of microplastics are released each time we wash them.

Tiny sea animals such as fish larvae and plankton ingest these microplastics, which means they enter the food chain. Scientists have dug deeper and found microplastics in the remotest of regions, such as the ice in the Arctic or deep down on the sea floor.

Every year, fashion brands are using more and more polyester, and this trend shows no sign of stopping.

Action: Invest in a microplastic washbag or washing machine that catches microplastics, and talk about this with a friend who might not know about microplastics released from clothing.

80   Get a job that helps the oceans

Working or volunteering to save the ocean can be an incredibly rewarding way to make a positive impact on our planet and marine wildlife. If you're considering a career change, or looking to do some advocacy in your spare time, here are some professions and activities to consider:

- *Underwater filmmaking.* If you want to get up close and personal with sea animals and tell the story of the ocean, consider underwater filmmaking. Your work can have a direct impact on public awareness of the ocean and can motivate other people to protect it.

- *Marine biology.* We can't hope to protect and preserve the lives of animals we don't understand, and that's where marine biology comes in. Marine biologists work with animals and other life in the sea and play a part in protecting everything from coral reefs to blue whales.

- *Ocean advocacy fundraising.* Fundraising for your favourite ocean advocacy group can be a great way to get involved with protecting the ocean in your spare time. You can simply ask friends and family to donate, or host a full fundraiser event.

- *Volunteer coordination.* This is someone who organizes and oversees logistics for groups of volunteers to help with ocean advocacy organizations. Volunteer coordinators may also be in charge of recruiting volunteers, which can be a great way to improve leadership and people skills.

- *Ocean engineering.* Marine engineers design and build marine equipment that can help with collecting data about the ocean, managing flood control on coastlines, and building infrastructure that protects marine animals.

81   Pick an ocean cause

The ocean is immense, and there are many different causes to support. Instead of being overwhelmed by the many different problems, try picking just one cause to work on.

There are different solutions to each problem, which means we need plenty of people using their unique skills to solve these ocean problems. Find one cause to support that you're personally passionate about and stick to advocating for it.

You can raise awareness about coral bleaching or marine plastic. You can advocate for endangered marine animals, or overfishing, or oil spills or rising sea levels.

Have a think and decide which cause you're the most passionate about, do some research and go from there.

82   Do humans have a connection to the ocean?

Life on Earth started in the ocean, which means all living beings can be traced back to an ancestor in the sea.

Humans have a connection with the oceans because we're part of their history.

Next time you're near the ocean, acknowledge the way you feel. Do you feel connected? Do you feel mesmerized? You might even feel a sense of fear and insignificance when you think of the vastness of the 'deep blue'.

But the ocean doesn't only serve a spiritual purpose – it's an essential resource for humans and land animals alike. Over half the planet's population depends on the ocean for their primary source of food. The oceans also give us water to drink through the rain cycle, give us the oxygen we breathe, and soak up the carbon dioxide in the atmosphere.

We need the oceans, and humanity's rise to power on this planet means the oceans now need us. We need to slow down, heal the damage we've done and renew our relationship with the oceans. We still can.

83 How to organize a beach clean-up

First check out no. 72 to find out if beach clean-ups really do make a difference. Hopefully, after reading this chapter, you'll feel motivated to host a beach clean-up of your own. Here's how you can get started:

- The first order of business is to identify a beach or area to host the clean-up. Check with your local authority if there are places that need volunteers to clean them up, or if you need any permission from landowners and so on. Permission to do a good deed for the planet? Annoying, I know! But this way you can make sure your clean-up is safe and hiccup-free.

- Next, you need to find some energetic and passionate volunteers – there's strength in numbers when it comes to cleaning up the Earth. Try to make a day of it by organizing a social event for people to attend after the clean-up. To spread the word, use social media and ask friends and family to take part or to ask others to join in.

- If you can, provide equipment for your volunteers – you'll need recyclable garbage bags, gloves and litter pickers. It also doesn't hurt to provide (plastic-free) snacks and refreshments, a first aid kit, sunscreen and extra equipment.

- The items you can expect to find will probably be a mix of recyclable and non-recyclable. Have your volunteers (safely) sort these items into different bags either during or after the clean-up.

- Make sure to pick a time when the beach won't be busy, like the early morning. And don't forget to have fun and feel good – you're doing an incredible service to our planet and its oceans!

84 How plastic nowhere near the ocean ends up in it

I had a dream once that I was walking on a busy beach, waves crashing to my left and children happily building sandcastles to my right. In the dream, I was content marvelling at the beauty of the sea, but suddenly the ocean transformed into a sea of plastic garbage. The beachgoers continued with what they were doing, and no one batted an eyelid. But I felt suffocated.

This kind of nightmare, unfortunately, isn't confined to my consciousness. The oceans are filled with marine debris, which is waste created by humans that has either intentionally or accidentally ended up in the oceans. Over 80 per cent of marine debris is plastic.[21]

Plastic litter thousands of miles away from the shore can also sometimes find its way into the ocean. It can go into local rivers and streams, which all eventually lead to the ocean. Plastic waste in landfill can also fly away into the air and end up in the ocean.

To end plastic in the ocean, it's not enough to not litter. We need to go to the source and turn off the plastic tap.

85 Does the ocean affect our health?

We rely on the ocean so much for food and water that if there are problems with the ocean, it can significantly damage our health.

Protecting the oceans from chemical spills, toxic algae blooms and harmful microbes ultimately protects us and future generations.

Chemicals such as mercury and lead that have been dumped or accidentally leaked can contaminate water or poison fish, which can have serious effects on human health.

Just as the ocean can negatively affect our health, it has positive effects, too. The ocean holds undiscovered medical solutions. So far, medicine has mostly been derived from terrestrial organisms. But scientists are increasingly turning to the ocean to treat difficult diseases like cancer and leukaemia, and to help with inflammation and pain management.

One example is a substance called discodermolide, which is thought to be released by deep-sea sponges to attack the rapidly dividing cells of a competing sponge.[22] This substance could potentially have anti-cancer properties.

The ocean profoundly affects our health. A healthy ocean can support healthy humans, and vice versa.

86   New technologies that could help the ocean

There are scientists and innovators working on new technology that could transform our relationship with the ocean from disastrous to restorative.

Let's have a look at some of them. Who knows, maybe you'll be inspired to come up with your own solution?

The Ocean Cleanup (https://theoceancleanup.com) is a company that collects plastic near the ocean surface into a net pulled along by two boats. The company is now working on improving designs to start cleaning up the Great Pacific Garbage Patch, which is a huge island of plastic floating in the Pacific Ocean.

Another company called Safety Net Technologies has created high-tech fish trawls that fishing boats can use to let go of unwanted fish. This has the potential to save the lives of millions of fish and marine animals that inadvertently get stuck in fishing nets.

Oil spills are another disastrous consequence of our fossil fuel dependence, and as long as fossil fuels keep being used, more oil spills will happen. There are some technologies being invented to clean up oil spills, such as clay sponges that draw out oil from water without harming marine life.

These new technologies are exciting, but we must be careful not to rely on them to magically save the ocean. It's much easier to stop polluting the ocean than it is to clean up pollution after the fact.

87   The consequences of a 2 degrees Celsius rise for the ocean

As of 2022, the planet has already warmed by just over 1 degree Celsius. International climate agreements have determined 1.5 degrees' warming as the limit to minimize the damage to life on the planet. But what will happen to the ocean if the planet warms beyond this limit?[23]

At 2 degrees of warming, not only will sea levels rise by over 50 centimetres (19½ in), but 10.4 million more people will be exposed to flooding than if warming was limited to 1.5 degrees.

Warming by 2 degrees will mean more carbon dioxide in the oceans, which will increase acidification and reduce oxygen levels in the sea. This means there will be even more low-oxygen areas devoid of marine life than there are now.

Fish and other species would migrate from their normal habitats because of changing temperatures. And those that can't migrate, like coral reefs, will die, greatly reducing biodiversity in the ocean. By contrast, at 1.5 degrees' warming, reefs could still survive.

If we limit warming to 1.5 degrees, some of the damage to marine species can be avoided.

88   Can we restore the ocean?

Even though we've subjected it to overfishing, acidification, oil spills and mountains of plastic pollution, restoring the ocean is still possible.

Sea life is remarkably resilient, and if we spend time and money this decade enforcing pollution controls and sustainable fishing, we could have a healthy ocean by 2050.

There are already signs of restoration efforts working. The proportion of marine species that are threatened with extinction decreased from 18 per cent in 2000 to 11.4 per cent in 2019.[24] Improved safety regulations in many countries have reduced the number of oil spills. Some seagrass meadows and mangroves have been successfully restored throughout Europe and the United States.

Restoring just 50 per cent of the ocean could cost the world at least $20 billion per year, would return $10 to the global economy per $1 invested, and create over a million new jobs.[25]

The ecological, economic, social, and yes, even spiritual benefits of restoring the ocean are undeniable. All we need is for our governments to make it a priority and take advantage of the narrow window of opportunity we still have.

89   Will we still be able to eat sushi in the future?

The earliest record of making sushi dates to the second century bce and was a way of preserving a valuable resource (this was about 2,000 years before the first refrigerator was invented). The fish used for this sushi was heavily salted and wrapped in fermented rice to keep it fresh. This rice would then be thrown away and only the fish would be eaten. Modern-day sushi in Japan is said to have been invented by the nineteenth-century Japanese cook Hanaya Yohei when he discovered that tossing rice with some vinegar and slightly marinating the fish in soy sauce made tasty, bite-sized food.

Today, sushi has exploded beyond the borders of Japan. You can find tuna rolls in supermarkets and cheap nigiri on restaurant conveyor belts around the world. But our world's sushi obsession is ravaging fish populations, and rising carbon dioxide in the sea is making survival for the remaining fish much harder, including farmed crabs and scallops which are struggling to create their shells in increasingly acidic water. Farmed fish such as salmon are fed soy, and soy contributes to deforestation.

The future of sushi doesn't look good, and it's unlikely sushi will continue to be as widely available as it is now. By 2050, fish like tuna will likely be off menus completely or become a luxury menu item.

Personally, I've (sadly) stopped eating sushi completely, and I invite you to do the same if you can.

References

1   World Economic Forum (2016). *The new plastics economy: Rethinking the future of plastics*. January 2016.

2   Li, W. C., Tse, H. F, & Fok, L. (2016). Plastic waste in the marine environment: A review of sources, occurrence and effects. *Science of the Total Environment, 566–567*: 333–349. ISSN 0048-9697. https://doi.org/10.1016/j.scitotenv.2016.05.084

3   Da Silva, R., Pearce-Kelly, P., Zimmerman, B., Knott, M., Foden, W., & Conde, D. A. (2019). Assessing the conservation potential of fish and corals in aquariums globally. *Journal for Nature Conservation, 48*: 1–11. ISSN 1617-1381. https://doi.org/10.1016/j.jnc.2018.12.001

4   Meijer, L., van Emmerik, T., Ent, R., Schmidt, C., & Lebreton, L. (2021). More than 1000 rivers account for 80% of global riverine plastic emissions into the ocean. *Science Advances, 7*(18).

5   Legresy, B. (2014). *Sea level: Understanding the past – improving projections for the future.* Commonwealth Scientific and Industrial Research Organization. https://research.csiro.au, last updated 22 September 2014.

6   Pacific Coastal and Marine Science Center (2020). *The Impact of Sea-Level Rise and Climate Change on Pacific Ocean Atolls.* United States Geological Survey, https://www.usgs.gov/, 22 October

7   The Ocean Portal Team & Bennett, J. (NOAA) (2018). *Ocean acidification.* Smithsonian Ocean, https://ocean.si.edu/, April 2018.

8   Laffoley, D., Baxter, J. M., Turley, C., & Lagos, N. A. (eds) (2017). *An introduction to ocean acidification: What it is, what we know, and what may happen.* International Union for Conservation of Nature.

9   FAO (2020). *The state of world fisheries and aquaculture 2020.* Sustainability in Action. Food and Agriculture Organization.

10 IUCN (2022). *The IUCN Red List of Threatened Species Version 2021–3.* https://www.iucnredlist.org. Accessed on 6 February 2022.

11 Jambeck, J. R., Geyer, R., Wilcox, C., Siegler, T. R., Perryman, M., Andrady, A., ... & Law, K. L. (2015). Plastic waste inputs from land into the ocean. *Science, 347*(6223), 768–771.

12 Break Free From Plastic (2020). *Branded Vol. III: Demanding corporate accountability for plastic pollution.* Brand Audit Report, December.

13 International Tanker Owners Pollution Federation Limited (2022). *Oil tanker spill statistics 2021.* January.

14 World Wildlife Fund for Nature (2019). *Solving plastic pollution through accountability.* March.

15 National Ocean Service (2010). *What is coral bleaching?* 15 March.

16 Watson, A. J., Schuster, U., Shutler, J. D. et al. (2020). Revised estimates of ocean-atmosphere CO2 flux are consistent with ocean carbon inventory. *Nature Communications, 11*(4422). https://doi.org/10.1038/s41467-020-18203-3

17 Alongi, D. (2014). Carbon sequestration in mangrove forests. *Carbon Management, 3*: 313–322.

18 Thiele, C. J ., Hudson, M. D., Russell, A. E. et al. (2021). Microplastics in fish and fishmeal: An emerging environmental challenge? *Scientific Reports, 11*(2045). https://doi.org/10.1038/s41598-021-81499-8

19 Danopoulos, E., Jenner, L., Twiddy, M., & Rotchell, J. (2020). Microplastic contamination of seafood intended for human consumption: A systematic review and meta-analysis. *Environmental Health Perspectives, 128*. 10.1289/EHP7171.

20 Cobbing, M., & Vicaire, Y. (2016). *Report: Timeout for fast fashion.* Greenpeace, https://www.greenpeace.org/archiveinternational/Global/international/briefings/toxics/2016/Fact-Sheet-Timeout-for-fast-fashion.pdf

21 IUCN (2021). Marine plastic pollution. Last updated November 2021.

22 De Souza, M., & Vinícius, N. (2004). (+)-discodermolide: A marine natural product against cancer. *The Scientific World Journal, 4*: 415–436, 11 June. https://doi.org/10.1100/tsw.2004.96

23 Jevrejeva, S. et al. (2018). Flood damage costs under the sea level rise with warming of 1.5C and 2C. *Environmental Research Letters*; Palter, J. B. et al. (2018). Climate, ocean circulation, and sea level changes under stabilization and overshoot pathways to 1.5 K warming. *Earth System Dynamics, 2018.*

24 Duarte, C. M., Agusti, S., Barbier, E., et al. (2020). Rebuilding marine life. *Nature, 580*: 39–51. https://doi.org/10.1038/s41586-020-2146-7, 2020

25 Barbier, E. B., Burgess, J. C., & Dean, T. J. (2018). How to pay for saving biodiversity. *Science, 360*(6388): 486–488. https://doi.org/10.1126/science.aar3454. PMID: 29724939, 4 May.

CHAPTER 4

FOOD

90　Reducing food waste is the number-one way to save the planet

If you've ever grown fruit or vegetables, you'll know how painstaking the process of growing from seed to fruit can be.

Plants that bear fruit or vegetables need plenty of water, healthy soil, space and sunlight. Now consider how much water, soil, space and sunlight are needed to grow food to feed billions of people.

A third of the world's food is never eaten.[1] That's a third of water, soil, space and sunlight that goes to waste. Food waste represents energy and resources that could have been put towards growing something else, or emissions that could have been avoided. Food waste emissions are huge: if food waste were a country, it would be the third largest emitter of emissions![2]

It's no surprise, then, that the climate non-profit Project Drawdown has found that reducing food waste is the number-one way to save the planet.

Action: For one week, try to write down everything that gets thrown out in your household. This can help you figure out which foods to stop buying, and if there's a pattern to the items that get thrown out the most.

91　Shop local, shop well

Globalization has made the world much smaller and made things possible that earlier humans could only dream of. It's allowed humans to travel and learn about cultures different from the one they're raised in. It means many products are cheaper to buy as we have access to countries that specialize in the production of a certain good. It means people living in Europe can eat avocados, and people living in East Asia can eat chocolate.

But the cost of this global interconnectedness is that shipping avocados from Mexico to Norway or cocoa beans from Ghana to Japan is very emissions-intensive, requiring huge cargo ships or planes which need fossil fuels to run.

If we shop locally, we send a signal to global food suppliers that we'd prefer they send fewer cargo ships and planes. This can then reduce emissions.

Action: Check out a local farmer's market or try to shop for seasonal produce that's grown locally.

92   The way to a better food system

The global food system is broken. Millions of people are routinely hungry and malnourished, even in countries where food is seemingly abundant.

Fast food is more accessible than fruits and vegetables in many countries. Fish populations are declining due to overfishing. Rearing cows for meat is ravaging the ozone. And we waste far too much food.

A better food system will need to accommodate for a growing population, urbanization and growing wealth, and work within the limitations of the natural resources we have.

There is no magical technology that is going to let us off the hook, but the good news is that the solutions are out there. We just need to implement them.

A more equitable food system might feature: community gardens in urban areas growing fresh produce; fewer pesticides and more regenerative agriculture practices being realized on a global scale; consumers eating less meat protein and more vegetable and insect protein; food waste compost collection for every household, and so on.

If you're reading this, you're one of the lucky ones. You're aware and have educated yourself about the problem and the possible solutions. We can have a better food system if more people are aware of how broken the food system really is, so your action activity for today is to tell someone else about what you've learned!

93 What can we learn from Indigenous peoples about food?

Indigenous peoples have been living symbiotically with the planet's natural systems for generations, and their food systems have historically been highly sustainable, nutritious and multifunctional. Indigenous food systems do not only function for food but also provide medicine, energy, and cultural and spiritual support. Indigenous peoples around the world have a knowledge of and connection with nature that's been passed down through experience, which means they understand the importance of respecting nature and maintaining crucial systems like biodiversity.

To be clear, Indigenous peoples still 'use' nature for survival, just like industrialized societies. But the key difference is that modern capitalist societies tend to exploit nature and take as much as they can to maximize profit. Indigenous societies understand that, to take, you must give back. This mindset is not inherent to capitalist systems, so we have to correct for it ourselves.

Think about it: when you buy vegetables from the supermarket, do you think much about the biodiversity of the soil they were grown in, who picked them, how much water they needed, and what will happen to the seeds and skins after you discard them? Considering and having gratitude for the origins of food is part of many Indigenous cultures and belief systems.

Unfortunately, Indigenous peoples are routinely left out of policy discussions, even though industrial farming and agriculture threaten these communities and food security on the planet. We can help by directly supporting Indigenous organizations, making space for their voices in government and also by listening and integrating some of their living philosophies into our own lives.

94   Is beef bad for the environment?

Even if you're new to the sustainability movement, you probably already know the answer to this question. The way we produce and consume beef today is disastrous for the environment.

Meat accounts for 60 per cent of all greenhouse gases from food production, and that's not all.[3] The average water footprint per calorie of beef is 20 times higher than for cereal grains and root vegetables.[4]

Cattle ranching also contributes to deforestation and forest fires. Some industrial farms will set fire to forests to clear space to rear cattle and grow soy for feed. This has catastrophic consequences for animal habitats and Indigenous peoples, who are often imprisoned or murdered for trying to protect forests.

It may be tempting to go for grass-fed or organic beef as an environmentally friendly alternative. While these methods may be more humane, evidence shows that grass-fed cows release four times more methane than grain-fed cows, because they take longer to reach an optimal weight for slaughter, so they emit more along the way.[5] Organic beef also has the same effect on the climate as conventional beef.[6]

Instead of using huge amounts of land and water to grow plants for animals to eat so we can eat animals, it's much more efficient to directly eat plants ourselves. This way, we can save water and trees, and be able to feed more people in the process.

We should all be trying to eat less meat if we can, and governments should be passing legislation to make plant-based food more accessible for everyone.

95   Palm oil: friend or foe?

Palm oil is a substance that has a bad sustainability reputation. Palm oil is vegetable oil that comes from the fruit of oil palm trees. It's produced either by squeezing the fruit or crushing the stone in the middle of the fruit.

Palm oil is in almost everything, because it does many different jobs and it does them well. For example, it improves the texture of many foods, makes cooking faster, and holds colour well. It can be used in foods but also in cosmetic and industrial products.

Because palm oil is in so many things, there is high demand for it, and farmers have an incentive to keep planting palm trees, often cutting down trees to make room for them. This means habitat loss for animals which use trees as homes, and also fewer trees to capture all the carbon dioxide we emit. Deforestation also sometimes infringes on the land of Indigenous peoples who often have no choice but to start working on palm tree plantations.

Replacing palm oil isn't easy, because other vegetable oils need more land for the same production of oil. That's why sustainable palm oil is coming into the mainstream, but that has its own problems as sustainability certifications aren't always clear-cut.

Palm oil is the perfect example of how difficult it is to achieve sustainability. It's a necessary ingredient in over 50 per cent of consumer products, and there's no ready replacement. Governments need to pass legislation to slow down the production of palm oil, or force companies to use other ingredients that are friendlier to the planet.

96 Let's slow down fast food

Fast-food restaurants are in total worth $798 billion, which is pretty much the same size as the global smartphone market.[7] In other words, fast food is a behemoth. Because it's such a large industry, any choice fast-food companies make environmentally has a huge effect on the planet.

The big problem with fast food lies in its name: it's too fast. Instead of the traditional dining model where customers sit down and use cutlery and plates that can be washed and reused, fast food is supposed to be convenient and quick, which requires disposable packaging.

Fast food also uses a lot of animal products. Think beef burgers, buckets of fried chicken, fish patties. This high consumption of meat and fish is bad news for the planet.

Again, because fast food is *fast*, animals need to be bred and fattened quickly. This means farming methods are usually less sustainable, more trees are cut down to make room for cattle grazing, and more methane emissions from all those cow burps.

Slowing down fast food means eating with intention and choosing ethics and sustainability over convenience and speed.

97　Donate to a food bank for the planet

So much edible food is thrown away every year, but what if this food was diverted away from landfill to stop hunger in low-income communities?

When organic waste goes to landfill, it creates methane, which is a potent and dangerous gas to be putting in our atmosphere. The food banks operating today reduce carbon dioxide emissions by 10.54 billion kilograms (23.24 billion lb) a year, which is the same as taking 2.2 million passenger vehicles off the roads.[8]

Around 811 million people were hungry in 2020, and around a third of food is wasted around the world.[9]

World hunger and climate change are both problems that it can be overwhelming to think about, but solving one can solve the other. Food banks are doing the much-needed work of solving both these problems.

As the climate crisis gets worse, food insecurity will increase. If we donate our surplus food, we can do our part in not making the problem worse.

98   What is food apartheid?

In the United States, 54.5 million people live in low-income areas with poor access to healthy and fresh food.[10] This is called a food apartheid. And it hasn't come about by accident.

For years, urban planning and redlining have favoured predominantly white, high-income communities. In the United States, these communities have on average four times as many supermarkets as predominantly Black communities.[11] Food apartheid refers to the systemic and racialized gap between those who have easy access to fresh, healthy food and those who don't.

This has implications for the long-term health of low-income, marginalized communities. It also decreases the resilience of these communities, as health outcomes are likely to be worse, especially in the aftermath of a natural disaster. Natural disasters will only increase with climate change.

If we want to fix this problem, the entire global food system needs to change. Most farmers around the world are women and people of colour. Non-profit food banks, on the other hand, are mostly white-led and operate in communities of colour. Food banks have been operating in low-income communities for decades, but food insecurity has only got worse.

There are lots of food activists who have created grassroots movements to feed and nourish communities until government and policy can step in. In particular, I recommend acquainting yourself with the work of Karen Washington (www.karenthefarmer.com/about), who coined the term 'food apartheid', and Ron Finley (https://ronfinley.com), a grower and food activist transforming empty lots in Los Angeles into gardens that produce fresh food. There is more about Ron Finley in Chapter 12: Plants.

99   How to ferment your own foods at home

Fermented foods like kimchi, sauerkraut, kombucha and yoghurt are trendy today, but before the refrigerator was invented, they were one of humanity's most important ways of preserving foods. Fermented foods are powerhouses for the gut, as they're packed with nutrients and healthy gut bacteria called probiotics.

Fermenting food is a clever and efficient way to preserve food that might otherwise go bad, saving food from going to landfill and nourishing your body in the process. It's also delicious.

You can ferment or pickle any kind of vegetable. I like carrots, cabbage and cucumbers. All you need to do is prepare and cut the veggies to your desired shape, and stuff them into a mason jar with some salty water (1 tablespoon of salt per cup of water) plus any herbs and seasonings you like.

The veggies will need to 'culture' at room temperature, which allows healthy bacteria to multiply. Taste the veggies as you go and once the tanginess is to your liking, store them in the fridge to be enjoyed for weeks and months. For an in-depth guide to fermentation, consider reading *The Noma Guide to Fermentation* (Artisan Publishers, 2018).

100   Soil biodiversity is really important for food

If we lose soil biodiversity, we lose food. Human populations are growing, which means healthy soil that supports plenty of food growth is more important than ever.

But because food demand is so high, there's pressure on agricultural companies to produce *lots* of food. And to produce *lots* of food, they need healthy crops that won't get damaged by pests or diseases. Which means they have a strong incentive to use pesticides or commercial fertilizers.

Here's the problem, though. Pesticides disrupt the balance of microorganisms in soil, which is bad for biodiversity. The fewer microorganisms in soil, the less healthy it is. Once you destroy soil health, it's very difficult to reverse.

Weather patterns are going to become even more unpredictable with climate change, but if we have healthy soils, our food production can be resilient. If we have bad soils, food supply might suffer.

Managing and looking after soils are the responsibility of farmers and governments, but it's in everyone's interest to keep soils healthy. As individuals we can help by adopting organic plant-based diets if we can afford to, and talking about the importance of soil biodiversity with our family, friends and political representatives.

101 The rise of urban farms

It's hard to picture urban metropolises like New York and Tokyo once being wildlife sanctuaries, but they were for millions of years until humans built concrete over the grass and cut down the trees to erect skyscrapers.

Today, megacities are often pretty much devoid of nature save for a few parks scattered around rich neighbourhoods. This lack of green space is posing a problem in a world of rising temperatures. The urban heat island (UHI) effect is a phenomenon that makes heatwaves even worse, as cities tend to be a little hotter than rural areas due to the heat trapped by building materials like asphalt, concrete, steel and brick which absorb the sun's energy.

Urban farming is one solution to this problem. Adding greenery to rooftops, walls and empty spaces can provide a significant cooling effect in a city. We need all the help we can get to protect ourselves against heatwaves, which have adverse health effects for vulnerable people.

Urban farms could also double as food supply for cities, which can help with cutting emissions associated with transporting food into cities. A win-win!

Action: Support a local community garden or urban farming organization, or why not try to start your own urban farm in your city? You can start an initiative in your office or residential building to grow some plants on the rooftop or walls.

102   Does beekeeping help the environment?

Contrary to popular belief, keeping your own honeybees doesn't necessarily help the environment. Some people keep honeybees under the impression that populating their area with busy pollinators will help the local ecosystem, but honeybees often outcompete other bees for precious resources like pollen.

Honeybees aren't the bee species most vulnerable to extinction, but they are the species humans are most likely to keep because of their honey. In North America, honeybees are the biggest threat to other wild native bees.[12]

The best way to help your local bee population is to avoid using pesticides in your garden (which could kill them), plant native flowers, and provide water in a shallow bowl for passing insects.

103   Food waste before the supermarket: a solvable problem

There are lots of ways that food is wasted before it hits the supermarket shelves.

Farmers in some countries are held to rigorous cosmetic standards for food: grapes that have to be the perfect size and shape and apples that must be blemish-free. Fruits and vegetables are often thrown away because they aren't 'perfect' enough for the shelves.

Cosmetic issues don't make up a huge portion of food waste, though. A lot of food at farm level gets wasted because of weather, pests and diseases, lack of labour to harvest produce, and fluctuating market prices for different produce.

The problem of food waste is complex, and it would take a whole book to work through the solutions. But it's important to be aware of just how many inefficiencies there are in our food systems, and that the food waste problem extends way beyond our own kitchens.

Because this kind of food waste is invisible to the end consumer, it's hard for us to understand the scale of the problem. But now, armed with awareness, we can vote for political candidates who can solve these problems, or donate to Indigenous food programmes which are doing a lot of the work to find solutions.

104   How much of food waste is at home?

In the United States, just under half of food waste happens at the household level.[13] Decreasing food waste at home is one of the most impactful actions you can take to help our planet. It might also be the easiest – all it takes is some advance planning.

You can plan out your meals in advance, and make shopping lists you stick to. You can make sure to freeze leftovers if you know you won't have time to eat them. You can also get creative with ingredients that might otherwise go bad in your refrigerator and so make a delicious meal.

Food growing takes a lot of energy, from the land to the labour to the fossil fuels burned to bring the food to you. When we waste food, we waste that energy – so let's all do our best to avoid that.

105   Best vegetables to grow from cuttings

The produce you buy at the supermarket can easily be regrown in your home and garden, so you have endless (free) supplies of the veggies and herbs you love. Regrowing your own cuttings also means you save some energy and food waste from going to landfill.

If you're busy and you don't necessarily have a green thumb, you can start with the veggies below. These are the simplest to grow from cuttings from vegetables and herbs you have left over:

- *Spring onions/green onions/scallions.* A delicious topping for almost any type of food you can think of, green onions are also one of the easiest to regrow. Cut off the roots, leaving about an inch of stem, and place them in some water. It should take about a week for the stalks to regrow, and at this point you can move them to soil and leave them in a spot that gets plenty of sunshine.

- *Basil, coriander/cilantro and mint.* Herbs are some of the easiest plants to grow. All you need to do is take a stem of the herb, leave it in a glass of water until roots begin to show, and then move it to a pot of soil.

- *Carrots.* Instead of regrowing the actual carrot itself, you can regrow the feathery carrot greens that sprout from the top of the carrot. Carrot greens are a tasty addition to pestos and salads, or as a replacement for spinach or parsley. Simply cut off the crown of a carrot, put it in water, and watch your greens grow.

106   Should we go back to seasonal eating?

When humans lived in agricultural societies, our only option was to eat fruits and vegetables that were in season. Indigenous peoples and people living in the Global South still eat this way. Eating seasonal produce has plenty of health benefits, and it can also be better for the environment.

Fruits and vegetables that are grown in greenhouses outside of their season can have a worse impact on the environment because greenhouses require a lot of energy. Produce grown in season consumes less energy because it doesn't need artificial light and heating.

But eating foods that are in season is only one aspect of a sustainable diet. Eating seasonal produce does have a lower impact but eating a plant-based diet is the most important choice you can make for the planet, seasonal or not.

107 How will farmers adapt to climate change?

As climate change becomes worse, seasons will be less predictable and extreme weather events will become more common.

Plants and crops will grow differently and more unpredictably, and harvests will be more at risk of damage. Farmers, especially those in poorer countries with no governmental support, are already feeling the effects of erratic weather.

For farmers to be able to adapt to climate change, biodiversity and soil health need to be prioritized. If soils are healthy and ecosystems in the soil are diverse, plants and crops will be more resilient to weather changes.

Some farmers are also using the same plot of land for multiple uses (e.g. crops and livestock together) instead of the traditional way of using a plot of land for just one use.

Some farmers in Brazil are involved in sustainable forestry, planting trees to clean the air, improve soil and even sell for timber in the future as an important source of income.

If there's one thing you can do to help farmers, it's to support organizations that protect soil. Consider donating to a biodiversity or soil health non-profit organization, preferably one that supports Indigenous peoples (who already do the most to protect biodiversity on the planet).

108   Is Big Dairy 'evil'?

When I did the research for this section, I came across a surprisingly sarcastic article about 'Big Dairy' on NMPF.org (NMPF stands for National Milk Producers Federation). The article called the phrase 'Big Dairy' one of the 'strangest terms attached to the industry' and went on to say that the dairy industry is in fact made up of a bunch of family-owned farms, not mega corporations.

The facts, however, are undeniable: between 2002 and 2019, the number of dairy farms in the United States decreased by 55 per cent, even though the volume of milk produced has increased.[14] This means there are fewer farms creating huge amounts of milk, which can only mean the farms are … big. So Big Dairy is not such a strange term after all.

In fact, according to the U.S. Department of Agriculture, more than 50 per cent of milk in the country is produced by just 3 per cent of dairy farms.[15]

Big Dairy is not great for the environment, especially because huge industrial farms are less likely to engage in regenerative agriculture than small family-owned farms. Dairy farming in general uses a lot of water and can also contaminate groundwater because of run-off from raising cattle.

Big Dairy companies have also spent millions lobbying against environmental regulations.[16]

So … evil? You decide.

109   Doesn't eating local matter more than going vegan?

Is giving up meat better for the environment than eating only locally produced foods? All kinds of meats and fruits and vegetables can be flown to us from all over the world, so isn't it better to eat local to cut down on all those transportation emissions?

Eating a plant-based diet over a meat-rich diet is much better for the environment than eating only locally made food (including meat). That's because transportation is only a very small part of the emissions created when meat products are produced.

For beef, emissions from transportation are responsible for only 0.5 per cent of emissions per kilogram produced.[17] The rest of the emissions come mostly from land usage and methane emissions from cow burps. Eating local meat doesn't make a huge dent in emissions but eating plant-based does.

110 What type of milk is the least bad for the environment?

Oat cappuccinos, almond matcha lattes, macadamia nut mochas ... Only a few years ago, coffee shop orders like this would have been unimaginable. But which one is the least bad for the planet? With seemingly endless milk options, it can be difficult to know which choice is the best for the environment. So let's break it down.

Dairy milk has by far the biggest environmental impact compared to any milk alternative. One glass produces three times more greenhouse gas emissions and uses nine times more land than any plant-based milk.

With plant-based milks, the environmental impact depends largely on the plants grown. Almonds, for example, are grown in arid areas that already have water shortages, and almonds require a lot of water to grow. Hazelnut milk is a tasty and nutritious alternative to almond milk without the water impact.

For a while, soy milk was the popular choice for vegans, and it's a solid choice, both nutritionally and for the environment. However, make sure the soybeans aren't grown in the Amazon rainforest – this just requires doing a little research on soy milk companies before you purchase. Large areas of the Amazon rainforest are cut down to make room for soy farms.

Hemp and flax milk are gaining in popularity as low-impact and nutritious plant-based milks. But the clear winner out of all the alternatives is oat milk. Oats are grown without the need to cut down any forests, and require less land and water than any other plant used to make plant-based milk.

Note: As with every piece of advice in this book, if you have a choice of milk that you love and that brings you pleasure, please enjoy it without any guilt! The purpose of this section is to educate so that everyone can make an informed choice and understand how broken our food systems are.

111   Easiest foods to grow indoors

Growing your own food is a wonderful way to get in touch with nature, increase your ecological empathy, and reduce emissions associated with food transportation! If you've wanted to get into gardening but don't have a garden, here are some plants you can grow indoors that also produce edible parts:

- *Chili peppers.* Pepper plants are perfect to grow indoors because they can't withstand any kind of cold. Make sure the pot is at least 20 centimetres (8 in) tall, and make sure the soil gets dry between watering. Pepper plants need plenty of sunlight, so put them near a window and eventually you'll get some delicious peppers to spice up your food.

- *Microgreens.* Plants like baby kale and arugula are packed with nutrients and are very easy to grow, with harvests ready in just a few weeks. Use small pots, using this rule of thumb: the larger the pot, the bigger the leaf.

- *Strawberries.* If you live in a country or area that gets a lot of sunlight year-round, you might want to consider growing strawberries. These little plants love plenty of sunlight and good drainage. You may get fruit once or even twice a year if you take care of these little treats!

112   Try to reduce takeout/takeaway

Getting food delivered straight to the door is a lovely luxury – with a few taps of a button, hot and delicious food arrives straight to our doorsteps. But this luxury is not good for the environment.

For food to be delivered in a good state, it needs to be transported in containers, usually plastic ones. Until there's a cheaper alternative to plastic, food delivery boxes are going to fill up landfills. It's worth mentioning that this is a systemic problem – it's not your or my fault that plastic is so ubiquitous.

However, we can still try to do whatever is in our power to reduce the amount of waste we produce. If you can, try to reduce the amount you order in. You can also ask local restaurants to consider using compostable or recyclable packaging. Often, restaurants need a little nudge from their customers to consider investing in planet-friendly practices.

113   Try out some insect protein!

You may soon be scooping insect protein powder into your cup after the gym. Insects as food has been the norm in many countries around the world, but it might be working its way into the mainstream in other countries for its stellar nutritional content and lower environmental impact.

Insects have a similar amount of protein to meat, plus a whole host of nutritional benefits.[18] Insects are also easy to produce, take up less land, and use less feed for the same amount of beef protein.

Plenty of countries that shun insects as food already eat crustaceans such as crabs, prawns and lobster, and crustaceans are genetically very close relatives of insects. So maybe instead of a lobster bisque, try picking up a mealworm fried rice. It's for the planet!

114   Is organic food better for the environment?

Since organic food is not made with pesticides, organic farmers must pay special attention to soil and regeneration to make sure their crops are strong. This means organic farming leads to healthier soils and more biodiversity, which is better for the planet than conventional farming.

According to research, buying organic meat isn't necessarily better for the environment. The emissions from organic meat and conventional meat (for beef and lamb) are very similar. Cows on an organic farm are reared more slowly, have more room to roam, and live longer, which is obviously better for the animals' quality of life but ends up costing the environment a similar amount.

If you can afford it, buying organic vegetables, cereals and so on means you can directly support good farming practices that take care of and give back to the Earth.

Legislation around organic food also needs to change to make it cheaper and more accessible. Everyone should be able to afford fresh, healthy food that doesn't cost the Earth.

115   The scourge of pesticides

Humans have been using pesticides for thousands of years to grow healthy crops. But what started as an efficient way to save crops and therefore food has turned into a chemical nightmare for the planet.

Pesticide residues are routinely found on produce sold in supermarkets, in animal feed, and in streams and rivers. Pesticides reduce biodiversity in soil, making it less healthy and resilient. The chemicals in pesticides poison and kill animals, bees and important pollinators.

Pesticides also severely affect the health of farmers, who often become poisoned from prolonged exposure to the toxic chemicals. But what can we do about this?

The government has the most control over whether the most harmful pesticides are banned, which means the best we can do as individuals is reach out to our politicians to advocate for less pesticide usage. You can also spread awareness about this yourself in your community.

116   Which fish species are most 'at risk'?

There are currently 22 fish species on the Greenpeace seafood Red List. These fish are at risk of being overfished or are irresponsibly farmed. If they disappear, they could disrupt the entire food chain.

It seems there aren't plenty of fish in the sea after all. Here are a few of the fish on the list that you can avoid buying:

- *Albacore tuna.* This tuna is usually canned and sold as 'white meat tuna'. Tuna are large fish, and they are one of the biggest predators in the ocean. Losing these fish has a knock-on effect on the rest of the food chain.

- *Cod.* This fish is popular in fish and chip meals: it's battered and fried and is practically a national dish in the UK. But cod is caught by trawling the bottom of the ocean floor, which can damage marine habitats and inadvertently catch other fish.

- *Atlantic salmon.* Atlantic salmon is either extinct or endangered in various areas of the world, which means most of the salmon that ends up on our plates is farmed.

Lots of salmon farms use pesticides and antibiotics to make sure the fish don't get sick, and the chemicals from the waste that comes from this process usually get released into the ocean. Salmon is often eaten for its health benefits because of the omega-3s it provides, but there's a chance that the chemical residues stay in the fish at the time of eating, which could undermine the health benefits.

117   The bottled water scam

Bottled water companies don't sell water, they sell plastic bottles.

Bottled water started gaining in popularity in the 1970s, after advertising campaigns by companies like Perrier made bottled water an aspirational product for sophisticated people. Bottled water is still popular enough that the market is expected to expand and grow for the next few years.

The problem is, for the vast majority of those living in developed countries, tap water and bottled water are identical in terms of quality. There are some exceptions to this, as seen in Flint, Michigan, whose residents are still awaiting justice from the government that allowed lead into their water supply.

Bottled water bottles are often made from plastic, which is made by using crude oil, which is a non-renewable fossil fuel. Millions of plastic bottles are used every day around the world, and many are not recycled. Many of these plastic bottles end up in the oceans, where they break down into smaller and smaller plastic particles.

As citizens, we can urge our governments to take action to enforce recycling schemes, or tax bottled water companies for their effects on the environment. As consumers, we can choose to avoid bottled water if we live in an area with clean tap water.

118   Can seaweed be a climate saviour?

Seaweed is a type of algae and has been harvested as food for humans for thousands of years. Seaweed is also great for the environment.

Algae is responsible for the oxygen in our atmosphere today, and seaweed specifically is thought to absorb around 173 million metric tonnes (191 million tn) of carbon dioxide per year, equal to around the annual emissions of New York State.[19]

Seaweed grows incredibly fast, which means it can absorb carbon at a fast rate. Long columns of seaweed also provide shelter for local sea animals, and there's evidence that algae and seaweed can reduce the acidification of the seas and oceans.[20]

Eating seaweed will increase the demand for seaweed, which means more seaweed farms and more benefits for the ocean and the Earth.

Even though seaweed is incredibly popular in East Asia, it's exploding in popularity in other countries. This could provide incentive for more companies in other countries to start seaweed farms, which would absorb even more carbon dioxide.

119   Make stock from fish and meat bones

Modern humans living in the Global North have built their entire lives around convenience and speed. For thousands of years (and today in Indigenous communities), convenience and speed were simply not considered. Survival depended on living in balance with nature and reducing food wastage.

For example, this meant that if you were eating chicken, throwing away the bones would have been unthinkable. Often, every single part of the animal eaten would be used for something.

Being sustainable can mean integrating some of these balanced ways of living with nature.

If you eat meat, try to preserve the bones to make stock. Stock can be made by simmering bones in water, with any herbs and spices you prefer. Doing this reduces food waste and provides you with a nutritious, delicious liquid to add to any future cooking.

References

1   World Bank Group (2014). Food price watch (English). World Bank, 1
    February.
    http://documents.worldbank.org/curated/en/931211468182366798/
    Food-price-watch

2   CAIT (2015). *Climate data explorer*. World Resources Institute.

3   Xu, X., Sharma, P., Shu, S., et al. (2015). Global greenhouse gas
    emissions from animal-based foods are twice those of plant-based
    foods. *Nat Food, 2*: 724–732.
    https://doi.org/10.1038/s43016-021-00358-x

4   Mekonnen, M. M., & Hoekstra, A. Y. (2010). A global assessment
    of the water footprint of farm animal products. *Ecosystems, 15*(3):
    401–405, December.

5   Harper, L. A., Denmead, O. T., Freney, J. R., and Byers, F. M.
    (1999). Direct measurements of methane emissions from grazing
    and feedlot cattle. *Journal of Animal Science, 6*: 1392–1401.
    https://doi.org/10.2527/1999.7761392x. PMID: 10375217, June.

6   Pieper, M., Michalke, A., & Gaugler, T. (2020). Calculation of
    external climate costs for food highlights inadequate pricing of
    animal products, *NatureCommunications, 11*(6117).
    https://doi.org/10.1038/s41467-020-19474-6

7   IBIS World (2021). Global fast food restaurants industry:
    Market research report.
    https://www.ibisworld.com/. Last updated 22 July 2021.

8   The Global Food Banking Network (2019). *Waste not want not:
    Toward zero hunger*. March.

9   FAO (2021). *The state of food security and nutrition in the world 2021*.
    https://www.fao.org/state-of-food-security-nutrition/en/

10 Rhone, A., Ver Ploeg, M., Dicken, C., Williams, R., & Breneman,
    V. (2017). *Low-income and low-supermarket-access census tracts,
    2010–2015*. USDA, 1 January.

11 Morland, K., Wing, S., et al. (2002). Neighborhood characteristics associated with the location of food stores and food service places. *American Journal of Preventive Medicine, 22*(1): 23–29. http://www.ncbi.nlm.nih.gov/pubmed/11777675 (3/05/11), January.

12 Curtin University (2021). Introduced honeybee may pose threat to native bees. *ScienceDaily*, 8 April. www.sciencedaily.com/releases/2021/04/210408131450.htm.

13 Buzby, J. C., Wells, H. F., and Hyman, J. (2014). *The estimated amount, value, and calories of postharvest food losses at the retail and consumer levels in the United States.* USDA, February.

14 MacDonald, J. M., Law, J., & Mosheim, R. (2020). *Consolidation in U.S. dairy farming.* USDA, Economic Research Report Number 274, July.

15 USDA (2012). *Farms, land in farms, and livestock operations.* NASS Publications. Summary available at http://usda01.library.cornell.edu/usda/current/FarmLandIn/FarmLandIn-02-19-2013.pdf

16 Lazarus, O., McDermid, S., & Jacquet, J. (2021). The climate responsibilities of industrial meat and dairy producers. *Climatic Change, 165*(30), 25 March. https://doi.org/10.1007/s10584-021-03047-7

17 Poore, J., & Nemecek, T. (2018). Reducing food's environmental impacts through producers and consumers. *Science, 360*(6392): 987–992.

18 Payne, C. L. R., et al. (2016). Are edible insects more or less 'healthy' than commonly consumed meats? A comparison using two nutrient profiling models developed to combat over- and undernutrition. *European Journal of Clinical Nutrition, 70*(3): 285–291. https://doi.org/10.1038/ejcn.2015.149

19 Krause-Jensen, D., & Duarte, C. (2016). Substantial role of macroalgae in marine carbon sequestration. *Nature Geoscience, 9*: 737–742 (2016). https://doi.org/10.1038/ngeo2790

20 P. Kaladharan, B., Johnson, A. K., Nazar, A., Ignatius, B., Chakraborty, K., and Gopalakrishnan, A. A. (2019). *Perspective plan of ICAR-CMFRI for promoting seaweed mariculture in India.* Indian Council of Agricultural Research, Central Marine Fisheries Institute, April, https://core.ac.uk/download/pdf/328922011.pdf

CHAPTER 5

HOME

120   Does turning appliances off standby really help?

Did you know that powering standby electronics is responsible for up to 1 per cent of global emissions yearly?[1]

This includes TVs left on standby (when the red light is on) and laptops and phones left on the charger even after being fully charged.

Until all our energy is renewable, turning off our electronics completely when we're not using them can be a small but impactful practice we can implement into our daily lives to save energy.

121   How much are our homes contributing to global warming?

Globally, roughly 29 per cent of emissions come from households, mostly for heating and cooling.[2]

It's very hard to make existing homes more eco-friendly, but even new homes usually aren't built to a zero-carbon standard.

Insulation is the most critical part of home building that needs to be improved. Better insulation means less energy spent on heating and cooling homes. Governments aren't taking this seriously enough yet, but there are some things we can do at home to decrease the emissions of our individual households.

By making sure heating isn't set unnecessarily high or air conditioning too low, using thick curtains to minimize drafts, and investing in insulation in your own home, you can help reduce the strain on our energy grid.

122   Want to skip the chemicals? Some DIY eco-friendly cleaning solutions

Living in a clean home is obviously a must, but sometimes sterility and hygiene can come at a cost to the environment.

Chemicals in some cleaning solutions like nitrogen, phosphorus and ammonia are not removed by waste treatment processes, meaning they can enter waterways and accumulate, disrupting the aquatic food chain. Some chemicals in cleaning solutions also accumulate in the air, contributing to smog.

Here are some DIY solutions that will clean your house without contributing to these problems:

- For an all-purpose cleaner, mix equal parts white vinegar and water, and a few drops of essential oil if you like to mask the vinegar smell.
- To deep-clean your dishwasher or washing machine, run your machines on the hottest cycle twice, once with vinegar and once with baking soda.
- To unblock drains, pour baking soda and white vinegar down the drain and leave it there for fifteen minutes. Then pour some boiling water down the drain – your drain should be unblocked!
- To clean glass, mix one part vinegar and four parts water in a spritz bottle to leave your mirrors and windows sparkly clean.

123   Fast furniture: an environmental disaster

Instant gratification is the defining element of the twenty-first century. We want everything next-day or right now; we keep our new items for a short period of time before throwing them out and buying the next trend.

Furniture is usually seen as an investment, but the category is the latest victim of the cult of instant gratification.

The rise of 'home tour' videos on TikTok and YouTube, plus an increased interest in home decorating during the COVID-19 pandemic, have fuelled a rise in 'fast furniture'. This term describes home goods that are produced quickly and cheaply, designed to be replaced when a new interior design trend takes over. Like the fast-fashion industry, fast furniture is often produced by low-wage workers overseas, using cheap, synthetic materials that aren't designed to last.

In the United States alone, around 11 million tonnes (12 million tn) of furniture are thrown out each year, and only 0.3 per cent of this waste is recycled. In 1960, only 1.8 million tonnes (2 million tn) of furniture was thrown out.[3]

Often, fast furniture is an accessible way for those on a low income to buy affordable furniture, so we shouldn't shame or judge these people for doing so. But this habit becomes a problem when we buy furniture unnecessarily, purely because it's cheap or because we want to hop on a new trend.

Fast-furniture companies should explore circular businesses, which could include buying back furniture after customers are done with it and creating new items to resell. As consumers, we can advocate for this change and also reduce the amount of new furniture we buy.

124   How many homes are ill-equipped for climate change-instigated natural disasters?

Extreme weather events are becoming more frequent as the climate crisis worsens, and data from the disaster relief charity ShelterBox shows that if these events increase at today's rates, 167 million homes globally will be lost between now and 2040.[4]

This is the equivalent of all the homes in the United States being wiped out. Storms, floods, wildfires, hurricanes – all these events will become more frequent and more destructive as our planet warms. We are not prepared to deal with the increasing frequency of these catastrophes.

Saving the planet isn't always about action. It's also about uncovering scary truths that propel us into action. The scary truth here is those 167 million homes. We have work to do.

125   How to compost at home

Composting is one of the most rewarding ways to reduce food and garden waste. When we compost, we reduce the amount of waste sent to landfill, which reduces methane emissions. It's also great to have compost on hand if you have a garden because compost enriches soil with vital nutrients and makes your plants healthier without needing chemical pesticides or fertilizers.

If you want to compost outdoors, get a compost bin:

- Place the bin in a dry spot away from direct sunlight.
- Start filling your bin with 'browns' – which are usually dry things like dead leaves, twigs, branches, cardboard.
- Then, slowly add 'greens', which are wetter ingredients like food waste, coffee grounds and fresh grass clippings. You should aim for this to be around 25–50 per cent of your compost pile.
- Turn your compost pile ideally every month to make sure there's enough air circulating through the pile.

For composting indoors, check whether any organizations collect food waste locally. Composting indoors is quite tricky, but there are some electric composters you can invest in which have made the process much easier.

126   Does saving water at home matter?

Earth is called the 'blue planet' because 71 per cent of it is covered by water. So why is water scarcity even an issue? Is it possible to waste water on a planet where water is so abundant?

Actually, yes. Humans haven't evolved to drink seawater. And, as it turns out, only 3 per cent of water on Earth is freshwater, and not all freshwater is drinkable for humans without treatment.

Water scarcity in an area depends on two things: how much freshwater is readily available near to where you live, and how quickly your local infrastructure can clean that water. If you live in an area where there are a lot of humans compared to the amount of freshwater available (which is the case in most urban areas), then saving water is really important.

By 2050, it's estimated that 57 per cent of people in the world will live in areas that suffer from water scarcity at least one month every year.[5] When water is scarce, every drop counts. So yes, saving water at home does make a difference!

Taking shorter showers, turning off the tap when we're not using it, not flushing the toilet unnecessarily – these are all impactful actions that add up, especially if everyone does them.

127   The world is … really noisy

For thousands of years, humans have woken up to the sounds of birds, streams, insects and rustling trees. After the Industrial Revolution, we created machines that have made our lives more convenient but which drown out almost every relaxing sound created by nature.

Sirens, car engines, trains, factories and construction are all noises we've accepted as part of modern life, but all of this noise is actually bad for our health *and* for the environment. Exposure to loud noise in humans increases the risk of high blood pressure, heart disease, stress and poor sleep quality.

Animals use sounds to survive – they use it to escape from predators, to find food, and to make their way through their environment. Loud noise pollution can affect their ability to do these essential tasks.

Noise pollution doesn't only affect land-dwelling animals. Human activity in the ocean such as the emission of sonar signals or deep-sea drilling can affect marine animals, too. Whales and other mammals that use echolocation to navigate might get interference from our noise, or lose their way and get stranded on beaches.

Tree planting and replacing fossil fuel-powered vehicles with quieter electric vehicles are two solutions that are easy to implement for our cities. More expensive solutions include investing in quieter road surfaces, installing noise barriers for train tracks, or designing buildings that absorb noise. We can vote or campaign for these policies as citizens in our respective countries.

128   How bad are fireworks for the environment?

Fireworks are beautiful. They represent celebration and happiness and give us an opportunity to stop and experience the moment. But at the risk of sounding like a party pooper, I'm here to tell you that fireworks are the most unnecessary form of pollution, and we probably need to say goodbye to them.

Fireworks release particulates which are four times smaller than a grain of pollen. These particulates are so small that we can breathe them in, contributing to health problems including reduced lung function and high blood pressure. They can also be released into the air, creating acid deposits (acid rain) that affect drinking water quality and wildlife.

Fireworks release smoke in amounts that rival wildfires, especially around big celebrations like New Year or the Fourth of July in the United States.

We've celebrated without fireworks before, and we can do so again.

129   Do we really need toilet paper?

Aside from being unhygienic, toilet paper use is responsible for rampant deforestation.

In many places in the world, a bidet or a bottle of water by the toilet is the norm to clean down there. Where I come from in Azerbaijan, the 'Western' habit of using toilet paper is looked down upon as … gross.

Not only is cleaning ourselves with water more hygienic, but it's also better for the planet. A bidet uses less water than toilet paper, and trees aren't cut down to make it.

Give a bidet a try – you may be surprised! Alternatively, there are lots of companies creating toilet paper from more sustainable materials such as bamboo.

130   Recycle your old electronics

We own more electronics than ever, and changing phones every year has become a common habit. But what happens to our old phones, laptops and TVs when we throw them out?

Most electronic waste comes from Asia, but Europe has the highest electronic waste generated per person.[6] When we dump our old electronics into landfill, toxic materials can leach into the soil and groundwater.

If we recycle electronic waste, not only can we divert these chemicals away from landfill, but we can reuse the non-renewable resources that were used to make the original electronics (like copper, aluminium, cobalt and silver). This means we use less energy to search for and mine these materials in the first place.

Try to use your electronics for as long as possible before upgrading, and after you're done with them, either give them away to family, friends or charities, or take them to a dedicated e-waste recycling organization.

131 Doing laundry the green way

Doing laundry is one of humans' most emission-heavy chores. It takes a lot of water and energy to wash our clothes, but the good news is there are actions we can take to make laundry a little more sustainable.

The first is to invest in an energy-efficient, green washing machine. Doing this has a hefty upfront cost, but your water and energy bills will be lower in the long term, and it's better for the planet.

If you can, try to opt for plant-based detergents, and look into investing in a wash bag to catch those pesky microplastics that shed from synthetic clothing (see No. 196).

The best way to reduce energy use associated with doing laundry is to wash clothes less often. A rule of thumb is that if there isn't any visible dirt or a bad smell, the item can survive a few more wears before washing.

132 Quick showers or relaxing baths?

The shower versus bath debate can be polarizing, but which is better for the planet? It all depends on a few factors. Is your shower head water-efficient? How long are your showers? Do you usually take a quick shower after your bath to rinse off?

Let's simplify it. If we're talking about one standard bath versus a quick five-minute shower, a bath usually uses, on average, around 5 litres $(1\frac{1}{3}$ gal) more water.

It's also worth noting that you can consciously reduce the amount of water you use in a shower by, say, turning off the shower head when you're lathering up. But water used while bathing is fixed – you can't use less. That said, you can reuse the water from a bath to flush the toilet or to water your garden.

Whether you're a bath or shower person, there are ways to adjust your routine to use less water, so there goes our chance of settling the debate.

133   Invest in a smart thermostat

We've created wonderful systems for heating and cooling our homes that don't require us to lift a finger. If it's cold outside, we don't need to wrap up – we just turn up the thermostat. If it's hot, no need for a cold drink – just put the air conditioning on to the lowest setting.

The trouble is, there's a lot of potential for human error when we adjust thermostats ourselves.

Investing in a smart thermostat can be a great way to reduce the emissions associated with heating and cooling your home. Smart thermostats monitor your energy usage and adjust automatically to save energy.

A smart thermostat will save you money on your energy bills and also reduce the emissions associated with heating and cooling your home. A win-win!

134   Insulate your home

Have you ever experienced a water bottle explosion in your bag because you didn't put the lid on tightly enough? This is similar to what happens when your home isn't well insulated.

You turn the heating on, ready to enjoy the warmth, but the heat leaks and escapes outside. So you crank up the heat even more, which means your heater has to work much harder than if your home was insulated.

Even small insulation fixes here and there can save energy and money in the long run. Try draft-proofing your windows or installing double-glazed windows. You can also use thermal curtains, or lay down carpets and rugs to improve floor insulation.

If you can afford it, insulating your walls and floors from the inside is a great investment to make for the health of your energy bills and the planet.

135 Switching to a green energy provider

I use a renewable energy company for my electricity, and not only are my bills lower but I feel a tad less guilty when I'm binge-watching *Euphoria* for the third time.

Check to see whether you can do this in your country, too – often, it's as easy as signing up with a new provider that handles the switchover for you.

Often, a green energy provider either invests in renewable energy for you, or they directly supply your home with solar and wind energy. Either way, switching your provider is a big message to send to fossil fuel companies that you *really* don't want their dirty energy.

If you live in a building where you aren't in control of where the energy comes from, see whether you can convince the owner or landlord to switch. Renewable energy is sometimes cheaper, which is a pretty good pro if you ask me.

136 Gas cookers: yay or nay?

Great chefs swear by gas cookers because of the control they give you over cooking. However, they have a bad environmental reputation.

The gas that comes out of spider burners is methane, which is much worse for the environment than carbon dioxide. Gas stove pollution is harmful to humans, and when we cook, it builds up inside our homes. If we open windows or turn on extractor fans, the methane escapes into the atmosphere.

Induction stoves are a better alternative to gas stoves – they're better for the environment, more efficient, and they still allow a lot of control over your cooking.

137   Always check for discounts

If you want to make the switch to more efficient domestic appliances like washing machines and dishwashers, sometimes manufacturers and stores will offer discounts for you to do so.

It's always worth checking to see whether stores will do this – some stores in the United States will shave $200 off the original price as an incentive for you to upgrade.

Switching to efficient appliances will save you a lot of money on your bills, and the planet will be much happier for it.

138   Use the power of the sun for free, clean energy

We have an object in our sky which is essentially a humungous ball of free energy. The Sun produces heat and light energy from the nuclear fusion happening inside its core, and some ingenious humans have figured out a way to harness and use that energy.

In some countries, you can get solar panels installed on your roof for free, paid for by the government. Getting solar panels installed means you get free energy during the day, which is usually the most expensive time for electricity.

Some governments will also directly pay you an amount of money for the energy you 'export'. This is unused electricity generated from your solar panels which is pumped back into the energy grid.

If you have a south-facing, diagonal roof, and your roof is unshaded during peak sun hours, then you could be saving a lot of money on your energy bills and contribute to the burning of less fossil fuel.

139   Switch to LED lights

Switching all the lightbulbs in the average UK home to LED lightbulbs saves up to 40 kilograms of carbon emissions per year.[7] That's enough energy to charge 4,866 smartphones.

LED stands for light-emitting diode, which is the most energy-efficient kind of lightbulb. LEDs use 90 per cent less energy than traditional bulbs, and they can last for up to 30 years.

They're a tad more expensive than normal lightbulbs, but they usually end up paying for themselves through lower electricity bills.

LED technology has come a long way, so you can expect the same warmth and quality of light as a traditional lightbulb, without the large energy cost!

140   Turn on the air conditioner early

On a hot summer day, it can be smart to turn on your air conditioning earlier in the day, before the noon sun beats down on your home. If you cool down your house before it gets hot outside, you can save energy.

The air conditioner will have to work much harder to cool down an already hot house, as opposed to keeping an already cool house at the same temperature.

It helps if your home is well insulated, too!

141   Use ceiling fans to your benefit

Whether it's hot or cold where you live, a ceiling fan can come in handy for saving energy while regulating the temperature in your home.

When it's cold outside and the heater is on, a ceiling fan can help the warm air that's accumulated towards the ceiling move to the rest of your home.

When it's hot, the air circulation from the fan can be a welcome reprieve and can have a cooling effect on your skin.

Ceiling fans can increase the effectiveness of heaters or air conditioners, without having to use too much energy.

142 Support the rights of climate refugees

At the UN Climate Change Conference (COP26) in Glasgow, no legal framework was agreed upon to protect those whose homes have been and will be lost to climate change. There is also currently no legally binding agreement for countries to accept refugees who have been displaced because of climate change. This means that for people who have fled their home countries because of extreme weather brought on by climate change, there are no legal protections. They aren't even recognized by the 1951 UN Convention on Refugees.

Climate change increases the risk of weather-related disasters such as drought, wildfires, storms, hurricanes and torrential rain. This most affects people who rely on the weather for their livelihood: farmers can lose an entire harvest or their crops can be destroyed, which means they're at risk of losing their homes; increased air pollution and dry air can increase the health-care costs of a family dramatically to the point of bankruptcy; or someone could lose their home to a hurricane or rising sea levels.

When someone's home becomes uninhabitable because of climate change, shouldn't they be allowed to start life anew in a different country? And be legally protected to do so?

The 21.5 million people displaced every year by the climate crisis usually come from countries which have the lowest emissions.[8]

Everyone should have a right to a home. And it's deeply unfair and unjust that those who are losing their countries and homes to rising sea levels and other climate-related disasters aren't currently being protected legally on an international scale.

143 Collect rainwater

If you live in an area with lots of rainfall, why not try collecting some of it in a bucket? You can use it to water your indoor plants, flush the toilet or even clean the floor.

Often, sustainability is about using what our planet gives us, and reducing waste as much as possible. By collecting and using rainwater, you can reduce the amount of strain your personal water usage puts on local water systems. It might seem small but doing something as simple as this can connect us with nature and help us think critically about the amount of water we use.

This is also an area where the government can step in on a larger scale. Authorities can give house building companies incentives to install rainwater collection tanks in new homes, which can be used to flush the toilet or be fed into hoses to use for gardens.

144 How our refrigerators contribute to climate change

It might start to seem like no aspect of our homes is immune from being bad for the environment, and refrigerators are no exception.

Chemicals used in refrigerants and coolants are toxic to the planet and air. These chemicals absorb heat and release gases that are harmful to the ozone layer. Once released, these gases can stay in the atmosphere for decades, and are very hard, if not impossible, to remove.

The gases trap infrared heat from the Sun, contributing to a warming effect on our planet. Some of these coolants are also used in air conditioners.

According to Project Drawdown (https://drawdown.org), 90 per cent of these emissions happen after the appliance has been discarded improperly. So, if you have an old refrigerator you're trying to get rid of, you should check whether it can be picked up by a local appliance recycling organization.

As with many contributing factors in the climate crisis, government regulation is essential here. In the UK and Europe, there are regulations that enforce proper appliance disposal, which isn't always the case in developing countries.

145 Grow houseplants that clean the air

Aside from relieving stress and providing company, plants in our home can also contribute to healthier, purer air.

The snake plant and the spider plant are examples of plants that can clear out chemicals like formaldehyde from the air and filter out carbon monoxide while also giving your home some more oxygen.

You might need more than just a couple of plants to effectively clean the air, but the simple act of owning a plant can serve as a powerful reminder that plants and trees are constantly doing important work that we can't see.

There may be environmental costs to the commercial growing of houseplants, however – see No. 357 in Chapter 12: Plants.

146 Homelessness and the climate crisis

As the world warms, the likelihood of natural disasters like hurricanes and heatwaves will become more common, and the most vulnerable to these are people who don't have adequate (or any) shelter. Not only are the unhoused even more exposed to climatic events, but climatic events will cause more homelessness.

Homelessness in general is a symptom of a societal problem, not an individual problem. But if we don't band together to help the unhoused, homelessness could be a death sentence in a warming world.

If you can, donating to a homeless shelter is a really great way to help. We should also be voting for politicians who prioritize solving homelessness.

147 Wash laundry at the lowest heat setting

Around 95 per cent of the energy used by our washing machines is for heating up the water that washes our clothes.

That's why lowering the temperature settings of our washing machines is a great way to save energy. In fact, washing your clothes at a setting just 10 degrees Celsius (50 degrees Fahrenheit) lower can use up to 38 per cent less energy.[9]

Washing clothes at lower temperatures also helps the colours and the fibres last a little longer than they would otherwise. So not only can we reduce the strain on the energy grid, but also on the clothes industry!

148 Skip the rinse before running the dishwasher

All dishwashers have food filters, so if you're looking for an easy way to save water, skip rinsing the dishes before loading the dishwasher.

Most dishwashers have sensors that analyse how soiled your dishes are and adjust temperature and speed accordingly. If you rinse your dishes, the dishwasher may not wash your dishes properly.

Simply scrape big bits of food off into your composter and make sure you wash your food filter regularly to keep your dishwasher running smoothly and to save energy and water.

149   Try to recycle but be sceptical of its effectiveness

You're probably familiar with the three Rs which until recently were the holy grail of sustainability: Reduce, Reuse, Recycle.

In a perfect world, everyone would do these three things and there would be much less landfill waste. But even if you recycled perfectly (which means washing food residue from containers, sorting paper from plastic, etc.), it's unlikely that all the items you put in the recycling bin would become new items.

If you live in the Global North, your recycling likely gets shipped off to other countries to be burned or sent to landfill. Countries that receive this waste are often overwhelmed and don't have the infrastructure to sort through items effectively.

This is a policy problem, and not our fault as regular citizens. We should still try to recycle, but we should place a greater emphasis on the first two Rs: reduce and reuse.

Recycling should be a last resort. What's more important is campaigning for better recycling initiatives and voting for politicians who care about these issues and want to transform how we manage waste.

References

1   Eden, S. (2012). The standby generation: Electricity low-power mode and sociotechnical change. *Environment and Planning A*, *4*(3): 509–512.

2   Goldstein, B., Gounaridis, D., & Newell, J. P. (2020). The carbon footprint of household energy use in the United States. *Proceedings of the National Academy of Sciences*. 20202020-08-11 00:00:0019122-1913010.1073/pnas.192220511711732.

3   EPA, *Durable goods: Product-specific data, facts and figures about materials, waste and recycling.* U.S. Environmental Protection Agency. https://www.epa.gov/facts-and-figures-about-materials-waste-and-recycling/durable-goods-product-specific-data

4   ShelterBox.org (2021). Climate crisis to destroy 167 million homes in next 20 years. Press release, ShelterBox.org, 9 June.

5   Boretti, A., & Rosa, L. (2019). Reassessing the projections of the World Water Development Report. *Clean Water, 2*(15). https://doi.org/10.1038/s41545-019-0039-9

6   Forti, V., Baldé, C. P., Kuehr, R., & Bel, G. (2020). *The global e-waste monitor 2020: Quantities, flows and the circular economy potential.* United Nations University (UNU)/United Nations Institute for Training and Research (UNITAR) – co-hosted SCYCLE Programme, International Telecommunication Union (ITU) & International Solid Waste Association (ISWA).

7   Energy Saving Trust (2020). *Buying energy efficient products: Lighting*, 5 October.

8   IMDC (2016). *Global Report on internal displacement.* International Organization for Migration. http://www.internal-displacement.org/globalreport2016

9   Home Energy Scotland, Save energy in your home. https://www.energysavingtrust.org.uk/sites/default/files/reports/EST_11120_Save20Energy20in20your20Home_15.6.pdf

CHAPTER 6
TRANSPORT AND TRAVEL

150   Are electric cars more sustainable?

In an effort to curb emissions and to make adjustments in line with the Paris Climate Accords, governments around the world are making pledges to subsidize electric vehicles and phase out fossil fuel-powered vehicles.

It's true that electric vehicles don't emit carbon while you use them, so they are a better option to reduce air pollution. But are they more sustainable overall?

If you're thinking of making the switch yourself, here are a few things to consider:

- Electric vehicles need … electricity. Consider how your country produces electricity: if it uses a lot of coal, then an electric car might have a negative effect on the environment as coal stations emit pollution to produce the energy that powers your car.

- The average electric grid in the United States, for example, runs on a mix of fossil fuels and renewables, which is a little better for the climate and makes an electric car a better option than in another country that uses coal for energy.

- The batteries that power electric vehicles need natural resources like cobalt and other metals. The world's largest cobalt deposits are in the Democratic Republic of the Congo, where workers including children use hand tools to mine the metal. Cobalt exposure is toxic to humans, so make sure you do your research on electric vehicle companies to make sure they ensure safe working conditions in their suppliers' cobalt mines.

Action: Making the decision to switch to an electric car is all about doing your research. And if you're outraged that you even need to do the research, let your voice be heard! It shouldn't be this way, and you can help change that.

151   The future of air travel

Flying is not great for the environment. Planes are basically huge jet fuel-burning machines that spit out a massive amount of carbon dioxide – and they're pretty inefficient.

Planes fly all the time, and on a schedule, whether they're full or relatively empty, which means it's hard to reduce emissions. In an increasingly globalized world, it's unrealistic to expect people to stop flying. But what does the future look like?

The biggest area of change likely to come in the next few years is the use of electric aircraft for short-haul flights. Short-haul flights have the highest potential for adoption of electrification and sustainable fuels, and they are the least energy-efficient flight routes. If we can electrify these routes, we can reduce a large chunk of airline pollution.

There are also some new technologies for swapping out jet fuel with other, more sustainable fuels such as biofuel. Biofuels use organic waste and are carbon neutral. These technologies are still in their infancy, and there are problems that still need to be ironed out before they go into wider usage.

For now, the technology for making aviation zero emissions is still being worked on. Until then, governments can levy a frequent flier tax and stop airport expansion. Some European countries are also campaigning for flight reductions on routes already supported by rail. Until sustainable flying is possible, we will probably have to settle for flying less for the sake of the planet.

152   Does low-impact tourism exist?

Going on holiday is often harmful for the countries we visit, but it doesn't need to be. Ecotourism is all about having a minimum harmful impact on the places we travel to.

Our planet is a beautiful place, and we should preserve its beauty for others to enjoy in the future. Tourism is a wasteful industry, partly because of the escapism associated with it. We visit another country for a week or so and quickly leave, and we don't need to confront the effects (both positive and negative) of our visit.

Here are a few easy low-impact actions to take if you're travelling:

- If you can, rent a bike or an electric car, and not a fossil fuel-powered car.

- Travel at off-peak times and dates to minimize strains on local resources.

- Avoid boat tours which use petrol and go kayaking instead!

- Take the train to your destination instead of flying, which can be a beautiful way to sightsee.

- Support local communities and businesses instead of big international chains.

- Travel with a refillable water bottle instead of buying plastic bottles at the airport.

153   What is *flygskam*?

Flygskam is a Swedish word which translates as 'flight shame'. It describes the feeling of eco guilt one gets when flying. The word became an everyday Swedish word after activists used it to discourage people from flying, thereby lowering their carbon emissions.

Swedish climate activist Greta Thunberg brought worldwide attention to the concept of giving up flying for the planet. *Flygskam* has been reflected in the travelling habits of Swedes and others around the world. In Sweden, the number of railway journeys has gone up and domestic airline passenger numbers have fallen.

Flygskam is an interesting social experiment in changing societal norms and how they impact our eco-friendly behaviour. It will be interesting to see what other social norms change in the next few years as the climate crisis worsens.

154   Let's make cities more walkable!

Since the advent of the car, cities and towns have grown bigger and less walkable. The United States has some of the least walkable cities in the world, which means it's hard to get groceries, access healthcare, and go to school or work without a car.

Walkable cities are much better for the environment and our health. Living in a walkable city can also combat loneliness as there are more opportunities to interact with your local community when you're able to walk around.

To make cities more walkable, there must be good-quality and easily accessible public transportation. That's why the most effective way to improve walkability in your city is to campaign for more investment in public transportation.

If public transportation is cheap, fast, accessible, good quality and reliable, then car driving is much less likely. Pedestrian and bike safety is also crucial for encouraging walkability, so governments should invest in wider pavements and dedicated cycling lanes.

As a citizen, it's within your power to voice your concerns about walkability to your local officials and make your opinions known at the voting or polling booth.

155   Private jets: a luxurious curse

If you think normal flying is bad for the environment, wait until you hear about private jets.

The super-rich are known for their jet setting – they can hop on a chartered plane at any time to go pretty much wherever they please.

In terms of fuel burned per passenger on board, private jets are extremely inefficient. A private jet is between five and fourteen times more polluting per passenger than commercial flights.

During the coronavirus pandemic, the wealth of the ultra-rich ballooned, and this has fuelled a record increase in the demand for private jets. The 400 richest Americans got 40 per cent richer during the pandemic, and this, coupled with a higher demand for 'minimal contact' travel, meant a 20 per cent increase in private jet travel in October 2021 compared to October 2019.[1]

If we taxed private jet sales and levied a tax each time a private jet took off, we'd probably have a lot of cash to invest in research for sustainable fuel technologies. (Sigh.)

156   The impact of business travel

For my last job, I used to travel from London to New York every few months to spend time with the team in the US office. I have friends who work in consulting who would travel to other US states to see clients on Monday and return on Thursday, every single week.

During the coronavirus pandemic, business travel stopped for more than a year. Neither my company nor the consulting companies imploded. Everyone carried on as normal. All that business travel we did before had been unnecessary ... and wasteful.

People who travel for business tend to fly very frequently, which racks up their personal contribution to carbon emissions, and even more so if they take business class, which is associated with five times more carbon emissions than economy-class seats.[2]

Business travellers account for as much as 75 per cent of revenue for airlines, so the industry would be unrecognizable if that disappeared. But the space left behind may leave room for another, better kind of travel to take its place – one that isn't focused on growth at all costs.

157   Cruises are horrible for the planet

In one day, a single cruise ship emits as many particulates as one million cars. Particulates matter are microscopic particles of liquid or solid matter that can cause respiratory problems in humans and animals, because they are so small that they're very easily breathed in.

The cruise industry is disastrous for the planet, and some ships are known to dump trash and fuel waste directly into the ocean.

I get it. Cruises are fun. You can watch the sun set over the horizon every day from a deck, you get to fall asleep to a gentle lulling of a ship, all sorts of amenities are right at your fingertips, and it's a great way to get to see many places in one trip.

But no amount of fun is worth sacrificing the health of the planet and oceans that support life on this planet. It's probably best to skip the cruise and stay on land.

158   How to have an amazing staycation

Sometimes staying at home or exploring your local area is the best way to relax and recharge.

Travelling can be stressful. A staycation can be a great way to discover yourself, uncover some hidden gems in your local area and reduce the emissions associated with travel. Here's how to have a successful staycation:

- Decide whether you want to stay home or book a hotel/getaway in your local area. Going somewhere else can be the perfect excuse to unplug and change things up a bit, without having to travel far. Just make sure to avoid using those wasteful hotel toiletries if you can!

- Be a tourist in your own town or city. Pretending to be a tourist and doing some sightseeing in your own town can renew your appreciation for where you live, and perhaps teach you something new!

- Treat it like an actual vacation. Rest and relaxation are essential for humans to be able to function at their best. Just because you haven't travelled to another place doesn't mean you can't relax like you would if you were away. Turn on your out-of-office automatic reply and delete those work apps on your phone.

- Do something special. Whether you splurge on a night out at a restaurant, run yourself a bubble bath, or try cooking a new dish at home, make it extra special and luxurious. Vacations are all about shaking up your daily routine and doing something to treat yourself. You deserve it!

159 The most picturesque train journeys

If you're looking to travel and see incredible sights from an unusual viewpoint, consider going on a train journey. Hopping on a train is a great way to see the scenic parts of a place without the emissions associated with flying. On a plane it's all about the destination, but on a train it's all about the journey.

- *Oslo to Bergen.* Journey along one of Norway's most scenic railways, with stunning views of mountains and fjords; you even pass by one of the filming locations for *The Empire Strikes Back* – the snowy mountainous village of Finse.

- *Istanbul to Budapest.* This train route will take you through four countries, starting in Turkey, then going through Bulgaria, Romania and Hungary over a week.

- *TranzAlpine New Zealand.* Starting off in Christchurch, this train will take you through the scenic and almost otherworldly landscapes of New Zealand, ending in Greymouth. The journey takes around five hours and is a great way to see the country's famous Southern Alps mountain range.

160   Offsetting your travel emissions

It's a comforting thought that every time we do something that might pollute the planet, we can just plant a few trees and the planet will be none the wiser. However, offsetting emissions has become a popular way for companies and governments to 'throw money at the problem' without making real change.

Aside from the fact that trees take years to reach maturity and start absorbing carbon, we're polluting the planet too fast for offsets to make a big dent.

Offsets can take the form of buying cleaner stoves for people in developing countries, or financing renewable energy projects that might not have enough funding. But it's hard to measure to what degree such offsets prevent emissions, if they prevent them at all.

If you do your research, there are some great companies you can donate to that are doing meaningful work in reducing the amount of carbon in our atmosphere.

Renewable energy projects need all the funding they can get, so buying offsets in this way can be impactful. It's important to remember, though, that our priority should be reducing emissions in the first place, and not relying on offsets as a save-all solution.

161   Bring your own bottle

Around six million people fly around the world every day. Each person on these flights needs to have access to water, and planes provide this water in plastic cups that aren't reused. If every single one of these people took a reusable water bottle onto the plane, imagine how much plastic could be avoided.

Granted, not every airport around the world has a water bottle filling station. And bringing your own bottle is a tiny drop in a huge ocean of plastic pollution. But small actions do make a difference, and behaviour change starts with you and me! If people see us bringing our own water bottles, they might be inspired to do the same.

162   Do eco-hotels make a difference?

Eco-hotels are becoming popular destinations for sustainably minded travellers who want to minimize their travel impact. An eco- or green hotel puts sustainability at the heart of the guest experience.

Every eco-hotel has a different offering – encompassing everything from 100 per cent renewable energy and water recycling systems to locally sourced ingredients and zero-waste policies. These hotels also often support their local communities by ensuring staff receive a living wage and providing opportunities for guests to give back.

It's fair to say that if every hotel operated under these principles, then it would make a difference. The traditional hotel industry is far from sustainable – daily towel changes and mini plastic toiletry bottles aren't exactly Earth-friendly.

If you are going to travel, supporting hotels that care about the planet and local people definitely makes a difference. Just make sure to do your research beforehand to make sure the hotel really is sustainable.

163   Combining travel with advocacy

One of the most rewarding ways to travel is to integrate advocacy into your trip. Tourism is often destructive or detrimental to local communities, especially in developing countries. Jamaica, for example, is a popular travel destination for Europeans and Americans. These travellers may be unaware that many local people in Jamaica are unable to access their own country's beaches without paying a fee to foreign hotel chains.

It's important to be mindful and respectful of your status as a visitor, and not confuse advocacy with 'saviourism' or see yourself as a liberator or rescuer of marginalized people.

In fact, the best way to be an advocate is to simply talk to local people, be curious about some of the issues people face in their daily lives, and learn the history and context behind why things are the way they are. This can give you the information you need to decide what kind of volunteer work would be most impactful for that specific community.

You can also raise awareness in your own country or community by talking about the issues you learned about (please don't take photographs of local people, though: they aren't props!).

164   Bachelor/bachelorette parties

In the UK, half of all flights taken by men aged 20–45 are for bachelor parties, or 'stag dos'. On average, men in the UK take part in four stag dos a year, most of them involving flying to another country.

Research has found that ten people going from London to Brighton instead of London to Barcelona cuts emissions by 98 per cent.[3]

Bachelor/bachelorette parties are a lot of fun, but it's possible to have just as much fun in your own country or town, or by taking a train to your destination instead. Consider this as an opportunity to get creative and find an unusual activity you will remember for a lifetime.

165   The inequality of travel emissions

Just 1 per cent of people globally are responsible for over half of aviation emissions. A recent study identified that the world's most frequent flyers travel the equivalent of three long-haul flights a year or one short-haul trip per month.[4]

Passengers in the United States have the highest aviation emissions, more than the next ten countries on the list *combined*. And North Americans fly 50 times more kilometres and Europeans fly 25 times more kilometres than those living in Africa.

Some activists have proposed putting a tax or levy on frequent fliers, to reflect the environmental cost of their non-stop flying in the price of their ticket. This could fix inequality of emissions without hitting the wallets of less advantaged, less frequent fliers.

166   The world's highest garbage dump

Mount Everest is a true wonder of our planet, towering at almost 9 kilometres (more than 5½ miles) above sea level. This marvel of nature should be treated with the utmost respect, but instead it's earned a reputation as the world's highest garbage dump.

Climbers have discarded camping gear, empty gas canisters and water bottles on the once untouched slopes. As the planet warms, old garbage that was previously frozen is beginning to thaw.

Officials around the mountain have now enforced a policy where climbers pay a fee and must bring down trash to get a refund. According to reports, however, climbers simply pay the fee and forgo collecting trash.

This is just one example of the negative effects of human negligence and dissociation from nature, and why having empathy for the Earth is so important.

167   The positive effects of wildlife tourism

Wildlife tourism has a very poor reputation, and for good reason. Often, wildlife tourism harms animals for the purposes of profit. But there are some wildlife tourism initiatives that can positively affect animals by providing funding for conservation, local employment, and much-needed education for visitors.

Wildlife tourism can also provide an economic incentive for countries or organizations to preserve, maintain and restore natural habitats. For example, the Thula Private Game Reserve in Zululand, South Africa, has a herd of rescued elephants that are protected from poaching and allowed to live in their natural habitat.

Visiting and staying at independent reserves like this one can be a great way to learn more about endangered animals and support the important work these organizations do. As always, make sure you do your research beforehand.

168   The cost of wanderlust

Humans are explorers. We're travellers and curious by nature, and travel can enrich us and expose us to new experiences that might help us grow or see the world from a new perspective. It's never been easier in human history to see all the wonders of the Earth – the rainforests, the deserts, the coral reefs, the savannahs – it's all there at our fingertips, just a flight away.

But it's important to weigh up the benefits of travelling against the cost to the planet and local communities. We must also recognize the immense privilege of being able to take flights and travel. Only 11 per cent of the world population took a flight in 2018.

'Catch flights not feelings' may be the sarcastic motto of the millennial generation, but it's costing the planet a whole lot. I propose we catch fewer flights, and we catch more feelings for the beautiful planet that we have a responsibility to preserve and protect.

169   Use reef-safe sunscreen

We need sunscreen to protect us from harmful UV radiation emitted by the Sun, but some sunscreens have toxic chemicals that harm wildlife in the sea and coral reefs. It's important to protect coral reefs because they play an integral role in the ocean ecosystem, including protecting our coastlines.

Try to use reef-safe sunscreen that doesn't contain chemicals that harm sea life. This is a list of some chemicals to avoid if you want to protect coral reefs:

- 3-benzylidene camphor
- 4-methylbenzylidene camphor
- benzophenone-1
- benzophenone-8
- nano-titanium dioxide

- nano-zinc oxide
- octinoxate
- octocrylene
- OD-PABA
- oxybenzone.[5]

170   Low-impact beach activities

There's nothing like a fun day on the beach, especially when you leave the beach better than you found it. We share beaches with hundreds of species of wildlife, so we should be mindful to enjoy activities that minimally disrupt the beach ecosystem. Here are some examples:

- If you love water sports, try to stick to kayaking, snorkelling or kitesurfing. Boats with engines emit greenhouse gases and disrupt sea life with noise pollution.

- If you encounter wild animals, try not to touch or feed them. Human intervention can disrupt natural ecosystems and biodiversity that are already fragile.

- If you make sandcastles, level them out before you go, as they can create obstacles for wildlife trying to get to the ocean.

- Try to leave pebbles, shells and rocks on the beach, too, as they provide shelter for small animals and shellfish and deliver important nutrients as they break down.

- Last but not least, pick up your litter. Once plastic litter is on the beach, it's guaranteed to make its way into the ocean, where it's difficult to pick up.

171   How to research your destination effectively

If you're travelling to a new country, it's important to respect its culture and traditions. However, it's even more important to be aware of how your presence in the country as a tourist might be contributing to injustice or harm to local people.

Here's a handy checklist of things to research to make sure your visit is ethical:

- Is your hotel a local business or a large international chain? Local businesses are more likely to respect local traditions and contribute positively to their community.
- Check whether the hotel mentions anything about the environment, and whether it seems 'greenwashy'.
- Check the history of how the country or city treats wildlife, especially endangered species.
- Do a quick Google search on the impact of tourism at your destination. Are there any stories of international chains participating in exploitation? Does tourism help or harm the local community?
- What is the record on human rights like in this country?
- What climate challenges does the country face and will you be contributing to them by travelling there?
- Are there any Indigenous populations in this country? How are they treated by the government?

172   Consider donating to local climate mitigation efforts

When you travel, research what locals are doing to help the planet or to help people adapt to climate change.

Often, the most impactful place to donate money is directly to people on the ground who are doing grassroots work to help their community. This approach also means that you can be sure your donation is going directly towards the people who need it most.

Different countries have different climate problems. For example, countries in South America might struggle with logging and deforestation, while those in West Africa might struggle more with droughts.

People who directly deal with the consequences of these climate issues are best positioned to find solutions. That's why sometimes it's more impactful to directly donate to local groups rather than to go through a third party or an NGO.

173   Different travel types compared

Transportation and travel often make up the biggest proportion of an individual's contribution to greenhouse gases. This means we have a lot of control over how much we individually contribute depending on the means of travel we choose.

Let's compare the different forms of travel (data based on UK typical emissions):

- *Walking or biking.* Zero emissions and plenty of health benefits. But you knew that.
- *Train.* Unless trains in your country are fully electric, your journey will emit 41 grams of carbon dioxide per kilometre.
- *Electric car.* This depends on your electric grid, and what kind of energy your country uses. In the UK, you're looking at around 53 grams of carbon dioxide per kilometre travelled.
- *Bus.* Though communal, most buses have huge engines that emit around 105 grams per passenger per kilometre.

- *Medium petrol car.* You're probably already aware cars aren't great for the planet, clocking in at around 192 grams of carbon dioxide emitted per kilometre.
- *Domestic flight.* Short-haul and domestic flights are the worst offenders for emissions, not least because there are other, more energy-efficient alternatives for these routes. A domestic flight will emit 255 grams per kilometre.[6]

174   What percentage of greenhouse gas emissions come from travel?

Around 24 per cent of global greenhouse gas emissions are caused by fossil fuels burned for road, rail, air and marine transportation.[7]

Over 75 per cent of these emissions come from road vehicles, and the rest come from planes and ships.

Transporting goods and people is crucial to our modern economy. This presents a challenge when trying to decrease emissions because we still need to preserve efficiency and speed to make sure the economy keeps going.

There are some other challenges to decreasing emissions from transportation. For example, it can be difficult to control the types of cars consumers buy. Even though electric cars are becoming more popular, road emissions have continued to increase because consumers are still buying bigger and heavier cars in the United States, Europe and Asia. Governments can and should encourage consumers to buy electric cars by offering discounts or lower taxes.

Aviation and maritime emissions are even trickier to decrease, as almost all modern ship and plane technology relies on fossil fuels. Our best bet is to decrease emissions where it's easiest to do so and tackle the rest later.

175   Are old cars better than new, electric cars?

Is a 20-year-old car worth keeping or swapping out for a new electric car?

Electric cars are greener than petrol or diesel cars while you're using them, but there are emissions associated with the production of electric cars. If you do buy a new electric car, it's important to keep in mind those emissions and weigh them up against the emissions of driving an existing old car.

A useful rule of thumb to follow when making this decision is that if you accrue high mileage, that is, if you drive a lot, then it might be worth investing in an electric car. If you tend to drive short distances only once or twice a week, then the emissions associated with the electric car's production might not be worth it.

Electric cars will only get greener as the energy grid switches to renewables. At some point, it will be worth investing in an electric car. But it's up to you to decide when that point is according to your lifestyle and needs.

176   Governments need to spend more on renewables

Fossil fuels are *so* last decade.

Even though they've fallen out of fashion, fossil fuels still account for two-thirds of energy subsidies around the world. Around a quarter of energy subsidies are for renewables, and the rest for nuclear.[8]

The technology for storing energy collected from renewables is constantly improving, which will account for fluctuations in energy provided by solar on rainy days, and wind on days with no wind. Renewables are also currently the cheapest source of energy, even when you account for fossil fuel subsidies.

All we need now is for governments to divert money away from the fossil fuel industry and towards infrastructure that will support renewable energy.

Renewable energy is going to take over the world, but it is governments that decide how quickly a country decarbonizes by deciding where public money goes. Keyword: *public* money. Which means that, ultimately, voters decide (hint: you).

177 How will self-driving cars affect the climate?

Imagine being able to hop into your car, be driven to your destination, and send the car off to pick up your partner from their workplace to bring them home. Driverless cars will be the 'chauffeurs' of the future, minimizing road accidents and reducing traffic and congestion.

We won't need to own as many cars, since cars can be 'summoned' or sent away based on the needs of multiple people, which will reduce the emissions associated with manufacturing cars.

It's also possible that driverless cars will reduce plane usage, because the prospect of being able to relax in your own private car while it drives you to your destination might be nicer than sitting in a plane.

There is a whole host of other benefits driverless cars will give us (especially if safety issues are minimized completely), but the environmental benefits alone are very exciting.

178 How easy is it to get rid of fossil fuel-powered cars?

In October 2021, the Mayor of London, Sadiq Khan, expanded the 'Ultra Low Emission Zone' (ULEZ) area to include Outer London. When I first heard the news, I was happy to hear the local government was taking steps to reduce air pollution in the city. The £12.50 per day charge would be enough to make people consider switching to electric to save money, which is great for the planet.

After reading what people thought of the change on Twitter, though, it was clear many people were upset. Local government, many argued, had imposed this tax burden on car owners without making any of the alternative solutions (like public transport) cheaper.

An ULEZ-style tax is one way for a government to reduce the amount of fossil fuel-powered cars on the road. But what if it wanted to get rid of them completely?

The government would likely have to spend a lot of money and resources to make other alternatives cheaper. They'd have to provide tax breaks for electric car purchases, invest in a charging network, and make public transport cheap and more accessible.

Many countries have put a ban on sales of fossil fuel-powered cars after a certain date (2030 in the UK), but there will be plenty of these cars left on the road. Getting rid of them probably won't be easy, but if you have the privilege to switch now, you can help the process move along faster.

179   Let's not travel *shame*, let's travel *change*

Global air traffic is set to double by 2037 to around 8.2 billion annual passengers.[9] Because planes aren't going to be electrified any time soon, this spells bad news for the planet. It's clear that, even with the knowledge that flights are bad for the environment, most people aren't deterred from flying.

In an increasingly globalized world, this is understandable. As incomes increase, people should be able to fly to visit family, or see new places and have new experiences that are usually restricted for the ultra-rich. Shaming regular people for flying, especially those who don't fly often in the first place, has the potential to alienate people from the environmental movement, and ignores some of the structural obstacles in place.

We can't forget that 1 per cent of people (approximately 80 million people in total) are responsible for over half of aviation emissions – this is where we should focus on changing behaviours.

The government has a big role to play in pushing changes in travel habits. Flights should be more expensive for frequent fliers and lower-emission modes of transport like trains should be much cheaper. The system is where we can productively focus our attention to make real and lasting change.

References

1 WINGX (2022). *Business Aviation Bulletin*, 3 February.

2 Bofinger, H., & Strand, J. (2013). Calculating the carbon footprint from different classes of air travel (May 1). World Bank Policy Research Working Paper No. 6471. Available at SSRN: https://ssrn.com/abstract=2272962

3 Euro News (2020). Nearly half of all flights from the UK are down to stag dos abroad. *Euro News*, 21 February.

4 Gössling, S., & Humpe, A. (2020). The global scale, distribution and growth of aviation: Implications for climate change. *Global Environmental Change*, 65(102194). ISSN 0959-3780. https://doi.org/10.1016/j.gloenvcha.2020.102194

5 NOAA. Skincare chemicals and coral reefs. National Ocean Service. https://oceanservice.noaa.gov/news/sunscreen-corals.html

6 BEIS (2018). *Greenhouse gas reporting: Conversion factors*. UK Department for Business, Energy & Industrial Strategy.

7 IEA (2020). *Tracking transport 2020*. International Energy Agency. https://www.iea.org/reports/tracking-transport-2020

8 Taylor, M. (2020). *Energy subsidies: Evolution in the global energy transformation to 2050*, IRENA, January.

9 IATA (2018). IATA forecast predicts 8.2 billion air travelers in 2037. International Air Transport Association, 24 October.

CHAPTER 7

FASHION

180   What is greenwashing?

'Our collection is responsible!' 'We have recycled plastic activewear!' 'We're committed to environmental responsibility!' 'We want to deliver the biggest impact in sustainability!'

Seeing these phrases peppered around on shopping websites might give you a sense of comfort – that the company you're buying from really cares. There is a growing awareness of sustainability among consumers, and it's slowly becoming a must for brands to be sustainable.

Since there's no regulation around the use of these terms, brands tend to use green marketing – which is essentially empty words without evidence – to make themselves seem greener than they really are.

This is called greenwashing, and it entails deceiving consumers into thinking a company's products or practices are more environmentally friendly than they are. I've fallen victim to this myself. It's so easy to get lulled into a false sense of security that governments and brands care when there are entire marketing teams working to convince us of that.

Greenwashing has become so bad that Earth Day, for example, has now become an opportunity for brands to push products or hold huge sales to encourage overconsumption. This can distract us from talking about very real issues around air and water pollution, and environmental racism, which is what Earth Day is all about.

Brands will often use social media to spread greenwashing messaging, posting pledges and running PR campaigns around their 'green' actions. By using green imagery and buzzwords, brands can portray an image of caring about the environment, without following through.

181   How to spot greenwashing

Until governments step in and regulate sustainability marketing, consumers will have to take everything with a pinch of salt. As the demand for sustainable products grows, so will the amount of greenwashing language we'll have to sift through. So how do we spot the culprits?

Look for numbers, not words. 'Sustainable' is just a word, but if buzzwords aren't being supplemented with tangible, measurable goals (usually listed on brand websites), then it's probably greenwashing.

Natural doesn't always mean good. Viscose, which is a fabric made from tree pulp, is a 'natural' fabric, but 150 million trees are cut down each year for viscose production.[1]

Vegan doesn't always mean good. Vegan is often synonymous with 'better', but vegan leather, for example, is plastic. Some brands will also unnecessarily add 'vegan' to their branding to make themselves seem more eco-friendly.

Check for certifications and a holistic approach. The brands that truly care will be addressing sustainability in every aspect – from manufacturing to sales to employment to fabrics. They'll be open about their processes (and perhaps imperfections) from the start, rather than brands which use buzzwords with no evidence to back them up.

Check out No. 189 in this chapter for green certifications to look out for.

182   Create your own capsule wardrobe

The culture and influence of fast fashion in society have made us all believe that we need the latest, trendiest piece to be fashionable. But creating a capsule wardrobe is one of the most effective ways to be stylish without relying on trends. Capsule wardrobes are timeless, catered to you and your style, and don't depend on fast-changing trends.

People are buying more clothes than ever before but keeping those clothes for almost half as long as they did in 2000.[2]

With a capsule wardrobe, the idea is to create a meaningful and thoughtful collection of clothes that you can mix and match to create endless outfits. This minimizes waste and overconsumption and also allows you to develop your own personal style rather than relying on trends.

To create a capsule wardrobe, make sure the pieces you choose:

- are suitable for the weather where you live
- fit you well (don't be afraid to get things tailored)
- work with your lifestyle
- are items you love and enjoy wearing
- are good quality and will last after multiple wears and washes
- are timeless and suit your personal style.

183   Influencers and fast fashion

The rise of social media platforms has fuelled a new type of marketing that had only been possible before with huge budgets: influencers. Brands are taking advantage of this new type of marketing by leveraging the personal relationships influencers have with their followers in order to sell products.

Influencers have a huge amount of power, and it's not uncommon for brands to sell out of inventory after partnering with certain influencers. Modern-day social media influencers are more influential than traditional celebrities, and there are more of them, which means there are more opportunities for brands to convince us to buy stuff.

Influencers project an image of a 'perfect' life that others can attain through buying the products they peddle. This creates a situation where people buy for the sake of buying, and influencers then quickly move on to promoting the next trend and the next new hot product to buy.

Fast-fashion companies are notorious for spending well into the millions on partnerships with (mostly women) influencers, while also severely underpaying the (mostly) women who make their clothes.

Do we need all the clothes influencers are pushing on us? Probably not. Should fast-fashion brands be producing less and focusing on paying their garment workers more? Absolutely.

184   Read your labels

Reading labels on food items or personal care products has become a common practice for those who want to know what they're putting in and on their bodies and whether the ingredients are safe. I'm a huge believer in treating clothing labels the same way, not only for the safety of our bodies but for our planet, too.

The skin is the largest organ in the human body, and most of us wear clothing treated with toxic chemicals and dyes and made of unbreathable polyester. We should be reading our clothing labels to know what we're putting on our bodies and the effects of the materials on the planet.

Producing clothes made with plastic materials like polyester and polyamide uses 342 million barrels of oil every year.[3] If we want this to change, let's start reading labels, demanding that brands do better, and pressuring our politicians to enforce regulations and change.

185   Skip Black Friday and shop small!

Black Friday is a shopping holiday observed mainly in the United States, when big brands offer deep discounts on their products. It's the biggest shopping day of the year, and big brands often take the holiday as an opportunity to encourage consumerism in order to boost their sales. Some big brands only 'go into the black', or begin to make a profit, during the Black Friday holiday season, after not making a profit at all throughout the year.

Black Friday can be disastrous for small businesses, which often can't afford to make deep discounts on their products. Small businesses have to be profitable to survive, which means they can't afford to operate at a loss all year just to make a profit one time. Sustainable small businesses are also often priced fairly to begin with.

Black Friday allows bigger businesses to get even more market share because they can afford to spend on advertising *and* give shoppers discounts.

Black Friday encourages overconsumption and impulse buying because prices are cheap, which means you're much more likely to buy items you don't need. Brands also usually offer free returns, and items are often sent to landfill after being returned.

If you can afford to, consider supporting a small business with your purchases and skipping big industry-wide sales.

186   We need to respect and protect garment workers

On average, it takes four days for a major fashion CEO to earn what a female garment worker in Bangladesh earns during her whole lifetime.[4]

Almost all garment workers are women who primarily live in the Global South. These women work in countries where workers' rights are either lax or non-existent, and huge fashion chains that are headquartered in Europe or the United States have taken advantage of this.

They produce their clothing cheaply by paying workers barely enough for them to get by. Many of these workers have no choice but to take these low-paying jobs in often unsafe working conditions, sometimes enduring abuse and harassment as they work.

The twisted injustice of all this reaches its peak around celebrations like International Women's Day. This is when swathes of T-shirts with #feminist slogans hit the shelves, made by an underpaid and overworked female workforce.

The people who make our clothes deserve to have a chance at a safe and happy life. Every purchase we make sends a message about the kind of world we want – if you can, purchase from companies that have proof of treating their workers well.

Our voices have power, too. Make use of social media to spread the word or talk about garment worker rights with people you know. And most important of all, vote for politicians who care about these issues. Bad PR around human rights abuses is a brand's worst nightmare, which means your voice has power to hold brands accountable.

187   Why is sustainable fashion more expensive?

When you buy sustainable clothing, you can probably expect to pay a bit more than you would for the fast-fashion equivalent. The rise of fast fashion has instilled in the consumer the belief that a T-shirt should cost the same amount as a sandwich. But low pricing makes it easy to forget the incredible amount of skill, labour and resources that go into making clothes, and that people and planet are often exploited to make the clothing cheaper for us to buy.

Sustainable fashion is often better-quality fashion. Fast-fashion brands tend to use cheap, low-quality materials that wear out quickly. Sustainable brands will usually seek out the highest-quality materials to make sure clothes last longer, which can hike up the end price of the garment. Sustainable brands will also usually pay fair wages to their workers.

Until consumers demand sustainability or governments enforce it, sustainability will be a niche market and therefore more expensive. Sustainable brands often can't take advantage of high demand to produce their clothes at a lower cost like huge brands can.

Sustainability is often associated with luxury, but should it be a luxury to buy good-quality fabrics stitched by people who earn a living wage?

Action: Try to support sustainable brands however you can. A purchase, a follow or a share can go a long way to increasing demand for sustainable goods.

188   The Aral Sea disaster

Once the world's fourth largest lake, the Aral Sea near Uzbekistan and Kazakhstan is now an arid desert with a graveyard of old ships.

In the 1960s, the Soviet government used the lake to irrigate farmland, and the practice continued well into the twenty-first century. The main crop the Aral Sea provided water for was cotton – which can use up to 20,000 litres of water to grow just 1 kilogram (900 gallons for 1 pound).[5]

The sea was used to grow so much cotton that it began to dry up, and it's now a tenth of its original size. This has spelled disaster for local communities, especially those which used to rely on the sea for their livelihoods.

The Aral Sea tragedy is just one consequence of the fashion industry's disastrous environmental effects.

189   Certifications to look out for

If you want to understand how sustainable a fashion brand is, look out for some certifications. If a brand is certified, it likely went through a rigorous process of being analysed for sustainability, which means it's guaranteed to be better for the environment and/or workers.

- *Global Organic Textile Standard (GOTS).* If a brand has GOTS-certified fabrics, this means you can be sure the fabric is organic and was made in an environmentally and socially responsible way. This covers the entire supply chain, from the way the plant was grown, to the protection of employees, to low water and energy usage.

- *SA8000 Social Accountability International.* The SA8000 Standard is a certification that guarantees the business treats its workers fairly, decently and ethically. Any business that has this certification has been vetted to make sure workers are being paid a living wage and working conditions are safe.

- *Fairtrade.* If a brand uses Fairtrade cotton, this means the cotton farmers who produced the cotton are paid well and work in safe conditions. Fairtrade cotton also ensures farmers receive extra money to invest in improving the quality of their lives.

- *B Corp.* A B Corp certification means that a company is legally bound to consider the impact of its business on workers and the environment. This goes against the traditional capitalist model, which only considers profit as a measure of the success of a business. If the company wants to stay certified, it must have a positive impact in non-monetary ways.

190   How much water goes into your clothes?

Vast amounts of water go into the production of our clothes. So much of the clothing we buy is either unnecessary or quickly discarded, which means a lot of water is wasted. Water that could have been used for drinking or growing food.

We use so much water for clothing production that it contributes to problems in areas of the world where water is scarce. Cotton is a particular culprit. Many of the word's largest cotton producers are China, India, the United States, Pakistan and Turkey, which are countries that have a high risk of water stress. This means the water resources in these regions aren't enough to meet water demand.

Every year, the fashion industry uses 93 billion cubic metres (121.6 yd^3) of water for clothing production.[6] This is enough to meet the yearly water demands of 5 million people.

As a society, we need to change how we value clothing. Let's try to value our clothes in terms of the vast natural and human resources that went into making them.

191   How to really shop sustainably

The main problem with fashion today is our ever-growing consumption of it. We buy too much and wear what we have too infrequently, and it's only getting worse as trend cycles become faster.

To really be sustainable, it's best to avoid buying new in the first place, but if you must buy something, here's a handy checklist of things to keep in mind:

- Do the 30 wears test before you buy. Will you wear the item at least 30 times? If so, it might be worth buying.
- Invest in clothing that goes beyond trends and that suits your personal style.
- Look after and repair your existing clothes.
- Check the material the clothing is made from. Is it high quality? Clothing made from natural fibres usually lasts longer.
- Ask brands questions when you aren't sure about the origin of an item or how it was made.

192   What happens to my donated clothes?

Doing a spring clean of your closet feels great. Putting your clothes into different 'donate' or 'keep' piles, feeling lighter once you've purged that pair of jeans you haven't worn in years. It can also feel good knowing that our clothes might be re-worn, or that the money made from selling them will finance the important work charities do.

We bring our clothes to the charity shop and they seemingly disappear into thin air. They become someone else's problem. And while charity and thrift shops do need donations to operate, they receive many more clothes than they can possibly sell. Our society's growing obsession with buying more than we need is unsustainable.

Many of these charity shops work with importers overseas who buy a large portion of our unwanted clothes to sell in local markets in various places around the world. If these clothes don't get sold off, they end up in landfill. These markets can also have a disastrous effect on local artisanal clothing makers who lose out on business.

It can be disheartening to realize that a good deed has negative consequences. However, it's never too late to change our ways and buy much less than we think we need.

193 The rise of rented clothing

Renting clothing is increasing in popularity as a way to get more use out of individual items of clothing.

Each piece of clothing in our closets needs to be worn a number of times to make the production worth the effort – ideally more than 30. But clothes are getting fewer wears, due to the rising stigma of outfit repeating, largely driven by social media.

While we shouldn't succumb to societal pressures not to outfit repeat, renting is a great solution if you need clothing for special occasions or holidays. Instead of buying and owning a fancy outfit you'll only wear once to an event, consider renting.

Renting clothes is better for the environment because it means fewer clothes are in circulation, and it's also great for experimenting with your personal style and understanding what you want to add to your capsule wardrobe (check out No. 182 for more on capsule wardrobes).

194   Why is fast fashion a thing?

The best way to understand why fast fashion exists is to think of it in the context of fast food. Fast food was created and popularized in the twentieth century to feed a new generation of workers – people who didn't have time to sit down and dine for long periods of time. It has prevailed to this day as a convenient way to get a cheap, quick meal that tastes pretty good.

The creation of fast fashion was a response to many different societal changes. Globalization and free trade allowed companies to produce clothes cheaply overseas, taking advantage of lax labour laws in other countries.

The rise of runway fashion in the 1990s and early 2000s created a new appetite for the democratization of fashion. Fast-fashion companies would produce similar runway designs for a fraction of the price. The response from consumers has been so positive that fast-fashion companies now release new products weekly.

As you can imagine, this isn't great for the environment. Fast fashion has perpetuated a cycle of fast-changing trends where designs are bought, worn and quickly discarded for a new style or trend.

195   What is the future of fashion?

Circular fashion is the future of sustainability in clothing.[7] Take-back programmes and zero-waste clothing will be a compulsory investment for fashion brands in the future.

It's hard to say how governments will enforce circularity in the fashion industry but being unsustainable will probably become expensive. Fashion brands will have an incentive to be more sustainable and to ensure there isn't any waste at any point in the fashion supply chain.

For consumers, this means no more trips to the charity shop to donate our old clothes. Our old shoes and clothes will be picked up by the same brands we bought them from to be reused and made into something else.

Reselling and renting will become much more popular, too. The technology for reselling and renting that already exists is still in its infancy, and it's not as convenient an experience for shoppers and sellers as it could be. But reselling and renting could soon become seamless and lightning fast for everyone, which will increase their popularity and usage in line with buying new clothes. This could mean buying new may just be reserved for special occasions and underwear.

Fashion could also become largely digital in the future. Augmented and virtual realities will give people the opportunity to dress their avatars or digital versions of themselves and wear basic sustainable clothing in real life.

All of these possibilities are really exciting for the planet and the future of the fashion industry. The Industrial Revolution gave us mass consumption and fast fashion, but the next wave of technological advancement might reduce the environmental consequences of our fast-fashion addiction.

196   Is recycled better?

Recycled fabric is becoming increasingly popular in fashion and footwear brands, but is recycled better for the environment?

Recycled polyester, or rPET for short, is usually made from recycled plastic bottles. This is a great way to divert plastic away from landfill and oceans and reduce the amount of petroleum we use to create virgin polyester.

Recycled cotton is also becoming more mainstream as a more sustainable alternative to conventional or organic cotton. Recycled cotton needs far fewer resources to produce, as it can be made using old clothes or fabric leftovers from factories.

Recycled is better than creating products from scratch. The problem with recycled polyester, though, is that it still releases microplastics when washed. To mitigate this, use a wash bag that can catch these fibres, or buy recycled items that don't need to be washed, like shoes or bags.

197   Plastic hides behind those names on clothes labels

Plastic in clothes has become mainstream in fashion as a cheaper alternative to natural fabrics like cotton, hemp and linen. Plastic in clothing releases microplastics when washed which then enter our waterways and oceans.

It can be difficult to detect when there is plastic in our clothes because there are so many different names for synthetic materials. Here are some different names for plastic in clothes:

- acrylic
- elastane
- nylon
- polyamide
- polyester
- spandex
- vegan leather (sometimes).

198   How to spot a fast-fashion brand

Fast-fashion brands have taken over social media and shopping malls, luring shoppers in with the promise of trendy clothes at low prices. As a former fast-fashion consumer myself, I know how enticing it can be to buy five or six new outfits extremely cheaply.

Fast-fashion brands depend on fast-changing trend cycles and our unwillingness to repeat outfits. They're also getting better at greenwashing. Here's how to spot a fast-fashion brand:

- The brand offers thousands of styles. Fast-fashion brands follow trends closely, instantly responding by making thousands of variations on different styles.

- The brand has short turnaround times for new styles. Fast-fashion brands have their eyes on celebrities' social media posts and fashion catwalks, ready to make duplicates of these clothes that hit sites almost the next day.

- The brand has limited quantities of particular garments. New stock arrives every few days, so brands want to get rid of old items quickly. This is how brands get shoppers to come back again and again.

- The brand uses cheap, low-quality materials. If a brand uses mostly synthetic fabrics, it's to keep costs low and profit margins high. These clothes are almost guaranteed to wear out quickly after a few wears and washes.

199   Buy second-hand

Second-hand shopping is already on the rise thanks to shoppers becoming more eco-conscious, and apps like Depop and Poshmark make it easy for everyone to sell their preloved clothes online.

Buying used instead of new reduces the amount of clothes in circulation, reduces pollution associated with producing new clothes, and diverts clothes away from landfill. It's not just clothes you should buy second-hand either – furniture, electronics and jewellery are all products that require substantial energy to produce from scratch.

It's important, though, to keep in mind that we can't buy our way out of consumption that is unsustainable in the first place. The most sustainable piece of clothing is the one already in your wardrobe. Reducing our consumption of clothing overall is the best way to be sustainable, but second hand is a great option if you need a new addition.

200   The importance of repairing

Have you ever taken up sewing? Tailoring and repairing clothes can be a great way to keep your closet as sustainable as possible.

As clothes have become ever cheaper, discarding that shirt with a hole in it and buying a new one instead is a much easier option for most people. However, if you repair your clothing, you save it from going to landfill for just a while longer. You also save money, keep your favourite items for longer and can get creative. Don't like a dress anymore? Turn it into a two-piece set! Got a hole in your jeans? Hem them and turn them into shorts!

Anything we can do to lengthen the lifetime of our clothing is great for the planet. Instead of throwing away or donating your clothing, think about how you can breathe new life into your wardrobe in a different way.

201   Cotton: the dirty crop

Considering how much we use cotton, it's a surprisingly difficult crop to grow. It needs lots of water, is fragile and if the weather is bad, an entire harvest can be ruined. But, worst of all, cotton is extremely vulnerable to pests.

This means that if farmers want to get a decent harvest, they need to use pesticides. To make enough money, farmers must expose themselves to these chemicals, often poisoning themselves or developing longer-term diseases from the exposure. Farmers also spend lots of money to purchase these pesticides in the first place, which can put them in debt.

Cotton grown with pesticides is conventional cotton, which makes up most of the cotton used today. We're not yet sure about the health effects of wearing clothing that's been grown with pesticides. If you have the ability, invest in organic cotton, for the good of the farmer, the planet and you.

202 The journey of a single pair of jeans

Denim jeans are iconic pieces of clothing, and what started as workmen's wear has quickly turned into the go-to casual garment of the entire planet. The denim fabric market size globally was around US$22 billion in 2021: it's a behemoth that doesn't show signs of slimming down.[8]

Denim fabric is a heavy material made from cotton, and its journey starts in the cotton field. The cotton is grown using lots of irrigated water and some pesticides to keep the crops free of disease. By the time enough cotton for one pair of jeans is harvested, it has used around 4,200 litres (1,100 US gal) of water. For comparison, the average recommended amount for you to drink in one year is around 730 litres (190 US gal).

The cotton is then processed in a factory where it's weaved into a thread that can be made into a fabric, and dyed, usually the classic indigo blue. It's then manufactured, cut and stitched into the right size and shape, and finally softened. This process uses around 500 litres (130 US gal) of water for just the one pair.

As you can see, denim jeans need a lot of water and resources to make. Once we start to understand *where* our clothes come from and *how* they're made, we can be more mindful and aware of our purchases and how they impact the resources we have on Earth.

203   Circular fashion is the solution

Circular fashion is the future and entails producing clothes in a way that regenerates natural systems, uses 100 per cent renewable resources and avoids waste. It means clothes never go to landfill, and when clothes reach the end of their life they're just remade into something new, in a never-ending closed cycle.

The way the economy works today is based on a linear 'take, make, waste' model, which is the least sustainable and most inefficient way to produce and consume goods.

We take natural resources from the planet, make products out of them, and then, when we're done with them, discard them and start the process again. There's no waste in nature, but humans have created entire societies based on creating waste, and it's so far been destroying the planet.

To ensure we can transition to a circular economy, governments need to put incentives in place for businesses. There are some businesses that already operate on this model, with take-back programmes set up to recycle clothes and footwear on behalf of customers. But these systems aren't perfect because the infrastructure isn't there, which is why government needs to step in.

204   What happens to our returned clothes?

Buying clothes online is easy, it's fast, and you can buy a whole outfit from the comfort of your bed. The only downside is that you can't try the clothes on, so why not buy two of each item in different sizes and then send back the ones that don't fit?

This is a common practice, but an extremely wasteful one. Online returns are increasing every year – currently at least 17 per cent of clothing is returned.[9]

What you might not know is that returns often end up incinerated or in landfills. It's a lot of hassle for companies to wash, inspect and repackage our returned goods, so it can be easier to just throw the clothes away.

If they can't be bothered to inspect the clothing, can't they donate the clothes instead of throwing them away? Donating items of clothing may damage brands' luxurious appeal, so most brands avoid going down that route. Designer brands are especially guilty of this – some have been caught out burning returned items.

Action: Before you buy an item online that may not fit, try asking the brand what they do with returned items. If they can't give you a straight answer, look elsewhere. The added benefit of reaching out to brands is that it signals that potential customers care about this issue, and might prompt the brand to reconsider their practices.

205   The fashion industry's emissions

Did you know that the carbon impact of the fashion industry is larger than that of the airline industry? The yearly greenhouse gas emissions of producing clothing and footwear are equal to around 2.1 billion tonnes (2.3 billion tn) of carbon dioxide emissions.[10] The airline industry – including passenger and cargo – emits around 1.04 billion tonnes (1.15 billion tn) of carbon dioxide.

Most of the emissions from fashion come from the production and preparation of different materials and fabrics. For example, the water used to grow cotton and the energy used to power the mill that makes it into a fabric.

Fashion brands also have a responsibility to improve their own processes. They can produce fewer clothes with more recycled materials or improve green packaging. These changes are simple and could take care of about 20 per cent of the reductions the fashion industry needs to make to fall in line with climate goals.

Action: Tell your favourite fashion brand how passionate you are about sustainability and ask them how they're improving their processes. You can do this by reaching out on social media or to customer service. It's in the brand's best interest to listen to their customers!

206 How to advocate for brands to have sustainable practices

As a consumer, what you want and demand has a lot of power. Companies can't exist without demand, and company practices can't continue if consumers don't approve.

If we want to make sure brands are sustainable, they need to know how we feel. One way to do that is to reach out to the brand directly and ask their customer service representatives for more information on what the brand is doing for sustainability.

Brands respond to bad PR, too. You can almost guarantee that a viral Tweet or TikTok video will get a brand's attention, so get posting if that's where your skillset is!

And, of course, never underestimate the power of your vote and your political voice. Brands and companies answer to governments, and governments answer to us. You have more power than you think.

207 Upcycle your existing clothes

Think of upcycling as breathing new life into your old clothing, saving it from landfill in the process. It can be a way to get creative, and to create your own unique pieces that speak to your specific style.

Upcycling is a sustainable habit you'll likely need some skills for – sewing specifically. But it can be a nice way to get creative and develop a new hobby!

So how can you start upcycling? To begin with, make simple changes to your old clothes. You can cut T-shirts to make them cropped or sleeveless, or add trims, patches or buttons, for example, to simple shirts. Use your imagination and what you have on hand, and you may be surprised what you can come up with.

You can also buy dye from your local fabric store and change the colour of your existing clothes. For example, if one of your white items of clothing isn't so white anymore, put it in the washing machine with some blue dye and you have a completely new item!

Upcycling is a great activity to do with kids to teach them skills like sewing, creativity and resourcefulness.

208   Buy less, buy better

Falling into the trap of buying 'trendy' items is something neither your wallet nor the planet will thank you for. There's a certain thrill that comes with buying something new, and brands capitalize on this feeling by creating advertising that taps into it.

Before I buy a new item, I like to play a trick on myself and force myself to wait 48 hours. If I really want something, I'll still want it in 48 hours, and by then I'll know if it's an impulse buy to get a temporary high, or if I really need the item.

Buying less and making investments (if you can) in high-quality garments means you can own clothes you absolutely love that will last years and still look great.

Remember, the most sustainable item of clothing is the one you already own. Get creative with what you already have in your wardrobe and you may be surprised!

209   Best and worst fabrics for the environment

Buying less and using what you already have in your closet is the best way to be as sustainable as possible. But sometimes we do need new clothes, and reading the fabric label is one way to make sure your clothing will last and that the material isn't harmful to the planet. Here's a list of fabrics to go for and ones to avoid:

Best:

- *Hemp.* This fabric was used by humans for thousands of years, and it's returning to the mainstream as a sustainable, healthy fabric. It can be grown anywhere around the world, requires very little water and naturally fertilizes the soil it grows in. It's one of the strongest natural fibres in the world and gets softer with each wash. It also doesn't need pesticides to grow and absorbs carbon from the atmosphere faster than trees do.

- *Organic or recycled cotton.* The whole supply chain of organic cotton has a lower environmental impact than traditional cotton, from how it is grown to how it is processed and dyed. Organic or recycled cotton biodegrades easily and can be a great source of cash for small farmers.

Worst:

- *Polyester/polyamide.* Polyester is a synthetic fabric made from crude oil, which means, if we buy polyester-based fabrics, we're increasing demand for fossil fuel production. These fabrics aren't biodegradable, they don't let the skin breathe, and they release microplastics when washed.

- *Traditional cotton.* Although traditional cotton biodegrades, it's a water-intensive crop and uses lots of pesticides in its growing process. Traditional cotton production is harmful to soil and local ecosystems. It's also bad news for farmers, who often have severe health problems because of exposure to toxic chemicals.

References

1   Sullivan, E. (2019). Fashion's impact on our forests. *Canopy Planet*, 21 January.

2   Remy, R., Speelman, E., and Swartz, S. (2016). *Style that's sustainable: A new fast-fashion formula.* McKinsey Sustainability, 20 October.

3   Ellen MacArthur Foundation (2017). *A new textiles economy: Redesigning fashion's future.* http://www.ellenmacarthurfoundation.org/publications

4   Vázquez Pimentel, A., Macías Aymar, D., Lawson, I., & Reward, M. (2018). *Work, not wealth: To end the inequality crisis, we must build an economy for ordinary working people, not the rich and powerful.* Oxfam, 22 January. http://hdl.handle.net/10546/620396

5   Maxwell, D., McAndrew, L., & Ryan, J. (2015). *The state of the apparel sector 2015. Special report. Water: A report for the global leadership award in sustainable apparel.* The Sustainable Business Group, September.

6   Ellen MacArthur Foundation (2017). *A new textiles economy: Redesigning fashion's future.* http://www.ellenmacarthurfoundation.org/publications

7   Ellen MacArthur Foundation (2021). *Completing the picture: How the circular economy tackles climate change.* http://www.ellenmacarthurfoundation.org/publications

8   Research and Markets (2021). *Global denim fabric market research report (2020 to 2026) – by application and region,* 25 August.

9   IMRG (2021). *Returns and refunds: The returning conundrum.* Interactive Media in Retail Group, June. https://f.hubspotusercontent10.net/hubfs/2182667/The%20 Returning%20Conundrum.pdf?__hstc=130162960.02a59a2a415 28649ea95b6725496d64f.1629358836575.1629358836575. 1629358836575.1&__hssc=130162960.1.1629358836575&__hs fp=1615285087&hsCtaTracking=02a098cd-64bb-4894-b0ec-59db322e5595%7Cd9be3341-9f7a-4c88-a97c-6718e84bb328

10 Berg, A., Granskog, A., Lee, L., and Magnus, K.-H. (2020). *Fashion on climate.* McKinsey, 26 August.

CHAPTER 8

CLIMATE JUSTICE AND INEQUALITY

210   What has inequality to do with climate change?

It's understandable to think that climate change will be a great equalizer, affecting everyone's lives no matter who they are. However, although climate change makes life harder for everyone, the consequences will be much worse for those whose lives are already hard due to their income, gender, disability, race, ethnicity and other factors.

Climate change is increasing food insecurity, reducing access to clean drinking water, worsening and prolonging droughts, and intensifying natural disasters like hurricanes. Disadvantaged groups are more likely to be exposed to and harmed by the negative effects of climate change, and they're also less likely to be able to adapt, cope and recover.

People living in countries in the Global South are already feeling the effects of climate change, even though people in developed countries on average have much more carbon-intensive lifestyles.

Inequality has everything to do with climate change.

211   What is climate injustice?

The people who contribute the least to the climate crisis will suffer the most consequences of it. That is climate injustice.

The climate crisis has made heatwaves hotter, hurricanes more violent, flooding more catastrophic, wildfires more ferocious and droughts drier. And things are only going to get worse as we keep filling up our atmosphere with greenhouse gases.

Low-income countries often don't have the infrastructure to deal with natural disasters safely, and these countries are also located in areas that are more prone to extreme weather events (Asia, Africa, the Pacific Islands, South America).

Any existing vulnerability will be made worse by the climate crisis, which means that those who are already struggling in our society will ultimately be worse off because of climate change. This is an injustice because those who are already struggling don't contribute much to emissions.

We need to make sure the most vulnerable in our societies are protected and given the tools to protect themselves and adapt to a crisis they didn't create.

212   Who will be the most impacted by climate change?

You've already experienced the effects of climate change. Climate change is not in the future: it's happening right now. But the extent to which it will affect our lives is completely dependent on where we live, how much money we have, how able-bodied we are and how generally advantaged we are.

The more your livelihood depends on the environment and weather, the more climate change will affect you. That's why Indigenous peoples around the world are most impacted by climate change. The same applies to communities that rely on agriculture or the sea.

People who are already vulnerable and discriminated against are also worse affected. This includes communities of colour (who in the United States are more likely to die from air pollution[1]), women, girls, the LGBTQ+ community (who in many countries don't have access to financial or legal resources because of their gender, gender expression or sexual orientation), and low-income people (who have inadequate protection against natural disasters).

213   Understanding privilege in sustainability

We live in a system that's built to extract the most profit from our planet and the beings who live on it. This system encourages us to buy things that don't last, and doesn't offer solutions for the waste that inevitably occurs as a result of our consumption.

Buying sustainable fashion is a privilege. Being able to offset your emissions is a privilege. Having the time to cook all your meals for yourself and your family is a privilege. Being able to afford an electric car is a privilege. Being able to have the time to think about how to be more sustainable is a privilege.

Not everyone has the good fortune to be able to lead a more 'sustainable' lifestyle. It's important not to feel guilty (or make others feel guilty) for not being perfect environmentalists. What is more important and worthwhile than ditching plastic straws is to change the system we live in – from an exploitative one to a regenerative one.

214   Where has climate change already hit?

The world has already warmed by 1 degree Celsius. During the last ice age around 20,000 years ago, the global average temperature was only 5 degrees colder than it is today, which should put that 1 degree into perspective. A few degrees make a huge difference.

Climate change is already here: glaciers are shrinking, ice at the North Pole is dwindling, seas are rising, rain patterns are changing. Island nations in the South Pacific like Tonga and Fiji are already feeling huge effects from climate change.

Rising seas are already destroying homes and displacing populations, and extreme weather events like cyclones are threatening the health of coastline communities.

Countries in East Asia are experiencing unusual torrential rainfall, flooding and extreme heat that leave millions of people vulnerable. In East Africa, droughts are now a fact of daily life for farmers. In Europe, flooding and heatwaves are threatening lives, and in the United

States, wildfires and hurricanes will only become stronger and more dangerous.

Climate change is here, and it's affecting the whole world already.

215   Sorry, billionaires, but Mars is a bad idea

'There is no planet B' is the rallying cry of environmentalists around the world. It's simple and obvious: we have only one planet. But when you consider that we use up all of Earth's resources for the year by the time July comes around, it's not a surprise that activists feel the need to state the obvious.

Billionaires, apparently, have a solution to our one-planet problem. Instead of preserving the planet we've already got, they're dedicating their wealth and time to assembling teams of scientists and colonizing Mars.

Colonizing a hostile environment like Mars will not be a walk in the park. It has no magnetic field to protect it from the Sun's radiation, which means people would have to live completely underground for protection from the dangerous rays.

Mars has lower gravity than Earth, which could spell all sorts of skeletal and cardiovascular problems for people living there long term. Not to mention, it's *really* cold.

Kickstarting a magnetic field on a planet 34 million miles away is an infinitely more complicated task than stopping a climate crisis on our planet.

It seems billionaires are unhappy with the world they've created, and are desperately trying to escape it, either through creating digital metaverses or through colonizing other planets. It remains to be seen how successful they'll be in their efforts, but there's no denying that the resources they're using for Mars would be much better used on Earth.

216 It's bad news that women aren't represented in climate

The average representation of women in climate negotiating bodies is around 30 per cent, even though 70 per cent of the 1.3 billion people living in extreme poverty worldwide are women.

Women also represent 50–80 per cent of the world's labour force in food production, even though they own less than 10 per cent of the land.[2]

Women are less likely to be literate than men, which means their options for employment are limited.

There's only one conclusion from these statistics: women are more vulnerable to the climate crisis.

If there are natural disasters like droughts or earthquakes, women are much less prepared for the financial implications of dealing with the fallout. And the climate crisis makes natural disasters more frequent.

If someone is experiencing hardship, it's only logical to ask them what kind of help they specifically need. Women not being included in climate policymaking means the solutions being drawn up may be inadequate to help other women adapt to climate change. And that's a huge problem.

217 What is environmental racism?

When communities of colour are disproportionately impacted by environmental health hazards, this is called environmental racism.

Civil rights leader Dr Benjamin Chavis first coined the term 'environmental racism' when he led a revolt against North Carolina's decision to dump soil containing toxic cancer-causing chemicals in a Black farming community in 1982.

He defined environmental racism as follows: 'racial discrimination in environmental policy-making, the enforcement of regulations and laws, the deliberate targeting of communities of colour for toxic waste facilities, the official sanctioning of the life-threatening presence of poisons and pollutants in our communities, and the history of excluding people of colour from leadership of the ecology movements.'[3]

Environmental racism persists today. In the United States, Black communities are 54 per cent more likely to live in areas with higher air pollution.[4] In the state of Louisiana, on a stretch of land dubbed 'Cancer Alley', the fossil fuel industry is trying to develop more petrochemical complexes that will double the cancer risk of the mostly Black residents living there. There are many more examples of environmental racism that could fill up entire books.

This injustice is not only happening in the United States. European countries also routinely ship plastic and electronic waste overseas to Africa or Asia, which exposes people in these countries to pollution and chemicals.

Colonialism and white supremacy have left a legacy of oppressive policies and laws that fail to protect the human rights of people of colour around the world. We must build awareness, support environmentalists of colour, hold our politicians accountable, and demand change.

218   What is ecocide?

We've already discussed how companies and entire countries are responsible for destroying and degrading nature for economic gain. Any human activity that destroys the environment or leads to the extinction of a species is called ecocide. For example, oil spills or mass deforestation could be considered ecocide.

For decades, activists and lawyers have been trying to get ecocide recognized by international courts as a punishable offence, similar to other international crimes like genocide or war crimes.

Do you think ecocide should be a crime?

219   Toxic masculinity is killing the planet

It can be argued that it's not a coincidence that we call Earth affectionate, maternal names like 'Mother Nature' and yet we still continue to exploit the planet. Toxic masculinity is so pervasive in our societies that it's possible that seeing nature as feminine might be contributing to its degradation and exploitation. Toxic masculinity sees anything feminine as 'bad' and glorifies destructive behaviour.

In fact, a 2016 study found that environmentalism is perceived to be a feminine behaviour.[5] Being caring and nurturing is associated with women, and caring for the environment goes under that umbrella. The research found that men generally didn't want to be seen doing 'green' things for fear of being seen as gay. Internalized homophobia hurts the planet, too – who knew?

This may be a surprising link to make, but in a patriarchal society men are raised to have less empathy. Empathy is an important quality needed to be able to care about the climate crisis. Stereotypically toxic masculine behaviours also harm the climate – for example, excessive meat consumption or driving oversized, fuel-guzzling cars.

The study also found that men were more likely to support eco-friendly marketing that featured mountains or wolves rather than traditionally 'green' or 'Mother Earth'-type messaging.

Empathy is a human trait, and nothing to be ashamed of. Toxic masculinity hurts everyone – and now we know it hurts the planet, too. Caring about the Earth and accepting that climate change is real is not unmanly.

220 The Chipko movement

An incredible success story of grassroots activism is the Chipko movement, a non-violent environmental movement started by women in India in the 1970s.

The Hindi word *chipko* means 'to hug'. Rural women in the Himalayan state of Uttarakhand would hug trees to protect them from industrial logging. Tree logging had been linked to floods that had killed hundreds of people. Trees protect against dangerous floods by absorbing water through their roots, leaves and branches. When there are fewer trees, flooding is more common and more violent.

As a result of this peaceful protest, the government abandoned their plans to continue logging. The Chipko movement inspired ecofeminism both in India and in the rest of the world, and is a testament to the power of collective, grassroots action. I hope it inspires you not to underestimate your own power to make change.

221 What is white saviourism?

White saviourism is the idea that disadvantaged people (often Black, Indigenous, people of colour, or BIPOC communities and those living in the Global South) need white people to 'save' them from poverty or misfortune. This idea is dangerous and rooted in white supremacy.

White saviourism ignores systemic causes for disadvantage such as colonialism and exploitation, implies that disadvantaged people are helpless or powerless, and ignores their voices, needs and lived experiences.

Being an effective ally to those suffering from climate injustice is not about 'saving' them. It's about recognizing how your privilege and voice can serve as an obstacle to justice and how it can take up space and drown out the voices of those directly experiencing the negative effects of climate change.

BIPOC communities and those living in the Global South already have the knowledge and agency to help themselves, but there are oppressive structures in place that often prevent them from implementing these solutions.

White people should be asking themselves: how am I contributing to ongoing systemic racism and climate injustice? How can I use my privilege to remove barriers to justice for affected communities? How can I amplify their voices and experiences and not my own?

222   What is seed sovereignty?

The way the farming and food system operates today is inherently extractive and exploitative and prioritizes economic profits over the environment, farmer and consumer health, and cultural food traditions.

Today, big agricultural corporations can apply for patents on seeds, effectively stealing and owning cultural foods that have been cultivated by Indigenous peoples for generations.

Seed sovereignty is emerging as a solution to create resilient seeds that are also culturally precious, and Dr Vandana Shiva, an Indian ecologist and environmental activist, is spearheading this movement. She created Navdanya (www.navdanya.org), which is an NGO that has created more than 150 community seed banks.

Seeds adapted to local culture are more nutritious, more resilient against climate change, don't need chemicals to grow, and improve biodiversity, which is why seed sovereignty is so important. Farmers grow food for the community, preserving cultural food and maintaining a sustainable relationship with the Earth.

Eating fresh, local and unprocessed food can be a way to support seed sovereignty, as well as supporting organizations like Navdanya which are doing important work to promote seed freedom.

223 Clean air should be a right

Everyone should have the right to breathe clean air free of pollution and toxic chemicals. The World Health Organization estimates that around 7 million people around the world die each year from air pollution. Many more suffer poor health consequences because of exposure to bad-quality air created by car fumes, agriculture, coal burning, and even the burning of fuels indoors for cooking.

In October 2021, the UN Human Rights Council made the historic decision to declare access to a clean and healthy environment a fundamental human right. The decision is not legally binding but is a move in the right direction.

Being able to breathe air should not be a privilege.

224 Why women in power bodes well for the planet

Countries with more female politicians have more ambitious climate targets. A 2019 paper written for the Climate Institute found that when women are leaders they are more likely to use their power to reduce emissions.[6]

This happens even in places where renewable energy isn't commonplace. For example, a women's mosque in India converted to solar energy as part of an effort to compensate for Uttar Pradesh's poor air quality and lagging progress in renewable energy.

The research shows that when women are fairly represented in a country's parliament and government, that country tends to adopt stricter climate policies. We have a lot of work to do to make sure women have fair and equal access to politics, and now we have another reason to move faster as a society.

225   Will taxing billionaires help save the planet?

Billionaires engage in carbon-intensive activities like space travel, flying in private jets and sailing in mega yachts, while engaging in climate philanthropy that, at best, makes them look good, and at worst, exacerbates the problem.

Philanthropic initiatives spearheaded by billionaires do little or nothing to address the inequalities and systemic problems that allow billionaires to exist. They also put the power of addressing climate change into the hands of unelected people.

Taxing billionaires can save the planet – the money could be put towards building green infrastructure, creating green jobs, and reducing economic inequality. More importantly, the money will be in the hands of (hopefully) democratically elected leaders who represent the interests of the public, not themselves.

226   The connection between colonialism and climate change

Is it a coincidence that the colonial powers of the twentieth century have some of the highest emissions per person today?

The wealth of countries like the United States, UK, France, Belgium, Italy, Spain and Portugal was and is still built on the exploitation of people and resources from other countries in South America, Africa and Asia. These countries are now experiencing the worst effects of the climate crisis, despite contributing fewer emissions.

For the sake of growing their wealth, colonial powers would often dehumanize Indigenous peoples to avoid feeling remorse for their oppression. Indigenous peoples were subjected to enslavement, torture, genocide and displacement from ancestral homes, all in the name of growing economic power and wealth for the colonizers. In the same way, colonial powers have separated humans and nature to justify exploiting nature for the sake of their own economic wealth today.

These countries must take responsibility for the crisis they have created by investing in a green transition and paying reparations to countries and people who have been colonized in the past and are now feeling the full brunt of the climate crisis.

227   The privilege of having a 'sustainable' lifestyle

So many around the world are struggling to access basic necessities like food and clean water, to make enough to support themselves and their families. Having the time and mental energy to think about climate change is a privilege in and of itself, let alone adjusting your lifestyle to be more sustainable.

In many developing countries, sustainability is a fringe topic of conversation. It's simply not on people's minds, because there are more urgent structural and economic issues to think about.

Plastic water bottles are widespread because tap water may not be safe to drink. Single-use plastic bags are often the only option at supermarkets, but being able to afford to put items in the plastic bag is a more pressing matter. Even worse, some countries don't allow citizens freedom of speech to advocate for climate action.

If we have the privilege, we should try to adjust our lifestyles to be more sustainable, while keeping in mind that there is no moral high ground for doing so. If we have the privilege, we should be using our political freedoms to push our politicians to make changes.

228 Community, not consumerism

In the twentieth century, psychology and advertising came together in the Global North to create 'the lifestyle solution', which was about prescribing consumer products as a medicine to solve life's problems. While human beings have always relied on, above all, community and social belonging to feel fulfilled and happy, in richer countries a culture of individualism has taken over, creating deep unhappiness and dissatisfaction. Consumerism has been portrayed as the cure for this unhappiness.

But every time we buy cheap products we don't need, we contribute to waste and injustice. We contribute to the exploitation of workers who make the product and to the depletion of precious natural resources. Consumerism is not the answer.

It's up to us to reject the consumerism that promises to be a replacement for social connection and community. In community, we can find love, belonging, tenderness, decolonization, liberation and healing. And, most importantly, we can find power and optimism, which will be essential in the push for climate justice.

229 You don't need to be a perfect activist

If you claim to want to save the planet but you use plastic, or you sometimes forget to recycle, or you sometimes waste food, drive a car, and occasionally eat meat, then you're a hypocrite and not a real climate activist – or so many people seem to think.

But the truth is you're a climate activist if you care about people and planet and want to help. It's not hypocritical to not be 100 per cent sustainable in your daily activities and still want to fight for a clean and healthy planet.

We're all doing our best within the limits of a capitalist system that is designed to exhaust us and separate us from nature. We need everyone in the movement for saving the planet, so embrace imperfection and welcome and include other imperfect activists as well.

230 We need to give Indigenous peoples land rights

Indigenous peoples are known to be one of the most effective groups at sustainably managing land and actively conserving nature. Despite this, land rights remain unrecognized for the vast majority of the almost 500 million Indigenous people on the planet.

When Indigenous peoples don't have formal legal ownership of land, they and the land become vulnerable to exploitation. If miners, cattle ranchers, palm oil companies or fossil fuel companies want to use the land for resource extraction, Indigenous peoples often have no say in the matter.

Research shows that when Indigenous peoples have strong legal rights to land, deforestation and carbon emissions decrease.[7] In 2020, the Standing Rock Sioux and Cheyenne River Sioux tribes in the United States successfully won a case to shut down the dangerous Dakota Access Pipeline. The Sioux Nation fought for land rights for decades, and it's certainly paid off for the planet.

Indigenous peoples have been safeguarding and conserving the Earth's biodiversity for generations. Securing land rights for them is not only the right thing to do, it could be the key to reversing the climate crisis.

If you want to help, start by supporting land rights organizations like Survival International (www.survivalinternational.org), the Forest Peoples Programme (www.forestpeoples.org) and the Indigenous Environmental Network (www.ienearth.org). You can also find out if you live on Indigenous land and create a land acknowledgement statement. I recommend checking out 'A Guide to Indigenous Land Acknowledgement' on the Native Governance Center website (https://nativegov.org) for more details.

231 Intergenerational inequality and climate change

Intergenerational justice is the idea that future generations deserve to inherit a clean Earth and healthy ecosystems, and present generations have a responsibility to make sure they do.

At the current rate, future generations may not have access to enough water or healthy soil to live a good life. They also may not get to enjoy the natural beauty of nature that is essential to maintaining good mental and physical health.

This is because present-day generations are sacrificing future generations' rights for the sake of economic gain today.

If governments commit to a green transition, and if we make changes to the way we consume, we can ensure our children and our children's children will be able to enjoy our planet just as we have.

232 Global warming will make the rich richer

The world's wealthiest countries are mostly in the northern hemisphere, where temperatures will stay relatively mild even as the climate crisis progresses. Those living near the equator will suffer the most from crop failures, droughts and extreme heat, while those in the Global North could actually reap warming benefits.

According to a 2019 study, richer countries that have contributed more to global warming have actually experienced increases in GDP, and the poorest that have contributed much less have experienced decreases in GDP.[8] The gap between the world's richest and poorest countries is 25 per cent larger than it would have been without global warming.

As global temperatures increase, real estate in rich northern countries will become extremely attractive, while homes nearer to the equator could become uninhabitable.

There are going to be huge winners who will profit from this crisis in the short term. These winners are people and corporations that already hold power in our societies and benefit from the oppressive and exploitative status quo. That's why it's so important we create a new system that balances out this power.

233 What does climate resilience look like?

Even though we should be trying to reduce emissions, the planet has warmed enough that some climate disaster is unavoidable. Climate resilience is about being able to prepare for and adapt to the negative or dangerous effects of climate change, and it looks different for everyone depending on where they live and what their livelihoods depend on.

In the Global North, governments will need to invest in infrastructure to protect people against flooding, wildfires and extreme heatwaves. This will include creating safe havens that provide air conditioning, heating and clean water to those who may not be able to access these amenities, and might also include planting trees on a massive scale in urban areas to mitigate extreme heat.

In the Global South, where the effects of climate change will be felt more often and more intensely, millions of people are extremely vulnerable and often live in cities that lack the infrastructure to deal with climate impacts. People living in the Global South are also more likely to work in agriculture, which means they are more vulnerable to losing their livelihoods if climate disaster strikes.

The main obstacle to climate resilience in countries in the Global South is funding. Only 3.8 per cent of global funding for climate change research is spent on Africa.[9] Rich countries that have contributed more to the climate crisis will need to provide aid money and funding to countries in the Global South to help them build climate resilience and invest in climate science.

234 Not everyone has access to green space

Getting out in nature improves your mental health. Studies show that even looking at a picture of nature can have restorative effects on the nervous system,[10] and that children who live in neighbourhoods with more green space are less likely to develop psychological disorders later in life.[11]

However, access to green space – and therefore better health outcomes – is unequal. Several studies in the UK and the United States have found that green spaces in urban areas are more accessible in white and wealthier neighbourhoods.[12]

Access to green space and the mental and physical benefits nature provides should not be determined by your race, income or education level.

If you are passionate about this, consider getting involved with your local community or government to push for change. Community action in some places has led to empty lots or parking spaces being transformed into green spaces.

235 Education as an antidote to climate injustice

Being educated gives people agency over their own lives, develops critical thinking, helps people become better citizens, and empowers individuals with the tools to help themselves and others.

When it comes to climate change, education can teach us to understand the limitations of nature and help us come up with creative solutions for safeguarding it. Education can also give marginalized people agency over their future and their lives, which is one way of achieving climate justice.

A report from Project Drawdown specifically recognized educating young girls in particular as a solution to increase climate resilience and reduce global warming.[13] This is considered more effective at reducing greenhouse gases than solar panels and electric vehicles, largely because the positive effects of the education spill over into their communities, improving health, natural disaster resilience and economic development.

236   Is anywhere safe from the climate crisis?

The threat of more heatwaves, floods, wildfires, hurricanes and suffocating air pollution is looming, and everyone living on this planet has reason to be concerned. Fear of an apocalyptic future might encourage some people to find the few places on Earth that are relatively protected from the effects of the climate crisis, but do such places exist?

The short answer is: no. Nowhere is protected from rising global temperatures. If you live in a landlocked country, you're safe from coastal flooding, sure, but you won't be protected from the effects of less rainfall and hotter heatwaves.

The only areas that are 'safe' are places where local governments have made a commitment to adapt to the climate crisis and invest in infrastructure to help protect their citizens against the inevitable.

237   What is climate gentrification?

I started Chicks for Climate (https://chicksforclimate.substack.com) when I was working full time in Shoreditch, a hip district in East London. Shoreditch is the ultimate symbol of gentrification, which is the process of a low-income neighbourhood being transformed by wealthier people moving in, often displacing local people in the process.

Wealthier people are attracted to lower-income neighbourhoods because of low rent and real-estate development costs. With climate gentrification, wealthy people are attracted to areas that are safer from the effects of climate change. For example, owners of coastal properties in Miami, threatened with sea level rise and rising costs of flood insurance, are moving to the historically Black neighbourhood Liberty City which is located on higher ground.

Climate gentrification can also happen when cities invest in green infrastructure. For example, introducing green space can increase property values and rent costs.

Governments need to support local communities and implement anti-displacement measures such as rent ceilings and long-term affordable housing. Otherwise, only wealthy people will end up protected from the effects of climate change.

238   Are capitalism and climate justice incompatible?

Capitalism has become a buzzword associated with societal ills. Plenty of people, younger generations especially, are becoming disillusioned with capitalism. Let's explore briefly if capitalism lives up to its bad reputation.

Most of the world lives under some form of capitalism, which is a system that prioritizes economic growth, consumer choice and innovation. The system has to an extent worked well – it has improved the quality of life of millions of people, made sure people have jobs to put food on the table and given us lots of technology that has improved convenience and communication.

However, capitalism prioritizes short-term profits and infinite economic growth – both of which are incompatible with living on a finite planet with finite resources. Capitalism doesn't have a framework to prioritize social or environmental interests. This means that companies and individuals will find the cheapest (and often most exploitative way) to make a lot of money.

In the United States and Canada, Indigenous peoples are often forcibly removed from their ancestral lands to make way for mining operations. In the Pacific, communities have been dealing with rising sea levels and poisonous oil spills for years already. These are just a couple of examples of the social and environmental costs that capitalism does not take into account.

If we want to enact climate justice (which means recovering from the climate crisis in a way that protects the most vulnerable in our society), then we must urge our governments to enact laws that force companies to consider the environment. If capitalism is to continue existing without leading us to extinction, we need to correct for the damage it does to the environment and people.

239   The importance of intersectionality

Hopefully by now you will have understood the key message that climate change does not harm everyone in the same way or to the same extent due to existing inequalities in society. Climate change will only make these inequalities worse if they are not addressed. Intersectionality, a term coined by civil rights activist and professor Kimberlé Crenshaw in 1989, describes how different categories of identity can intersect to create multiple forms of discrimination. Race, gender, ethnicity, disability, income, country of origin, class and more interact and create different experiences of climate injustice and discrimination.

Climate solutions are not just about recycling and installing solar panels. They are also about dismantling underlying forces of oppression and inequality and including marginalized identities in climate policymaking. Social justice and climate justice go hand in hand.

If you're interested in finding out more about this, I recommend checking out the organization Intersectional Environmentalist (www. intersectionalenvironmentalist.com) founded by Leah Thomas, which aims to amplify the voices of the unheard in the environmental justice movement.

References

1   Qian Di, M. S., et al. (2017). Air pollution and mortality in the Medicare population. *The New England Journal of Medicine, 376*(26): 2513–2522.

2   Osman-Elasha, B. Women ... In the shadow of climate change, *UN Chronicle.* https://www.un.org/en/chronicle/article/womenin-shadow-climate-change

3   Chavis, Benjamin F. (1993). 'Foreword', *Confronting Environmental Racism, Voices from the Grassroots.* Robert D. Bullard, 3–5.

4   Mikati, I., Benson, A. F., Luben, T. J., Sacks, J. D., and Richmond-Bryant, J. (2018). Disparities in distribution of particulate matter emission sources by race and poverty status, *American Journal of Public Health, 108*: 480–485. https://doi.org/10.2105/AJPH.2017.304297

5   Brough, A. R., Wilkie, J. E. B., Ma, J., Isaac, M. S., & Gal, D. (2016). Is eco-friendly unmanly? The green-feminine stereotype and its effect on sustainable consumption. *Journal of Consumer Research, 43*(4): 567–582. https://doi.org/10.1093/jcr/ucw044

6   Collins, C. (2019). *Can improving women's representation in environmental governance reduce greenhouse gas emissions?* Climate Institute.

7   Etchart, L. (2017). The role of indigenous peoples in combating climate change. *Palgrave Communications, 3*(17085). https://doi.org/10.1057/palcomms.2017.85

8   Diffenbaugh, N. S., & Burke, M. (2019). Global warming has increased global economic inequality. *Proceedings of the National Academy of Sciences*, 14 May. 00:00:009808-981310.1073/pnas.181602011611620

9   Overland, I., Sagbakken, H. F., Isataeva, A., Kolodzinskaia, G., Simpson, N. P., Trisos, C., & Vakulchuk, R. (2021). Funding flows for climate change research on Africa: Where do they come from and where do they go? *Climate and Development*. https://doi.org/10.1080/17565529.2021.1976609

10 Van den Berg, M. M. H. E., et al. (2015). Autonomic nervous system responses to viewing green and built settings: Differentiating between sympathetic and parasympathetic activity. *International Journal of Environmental Research and Public Health*, *12*(12): 15860–15874. https://doi.org/10.3390/ijerph121215026

11 Engemann, K., Pedersen, C. B., Arge, L., & Svenning, J.-C. (2019). Residential green space in childhood is associated with lower risk of psychiatric disorders from adolescence into adulthood. *Proceedings of the National Academy of Sciences*. 20192019-03-12 00:00:005188-519310.1073/pnas.180750411611611

12 Nesbitt, L., Meitner, M. J., Girling, C., Sheppard, S. R. J., & Lu, Y. (2019). Who has access to urban vegetation? A spatial analysis of distributional green equity in 10 US cities. *Landscape and Urban Planning*, *181*: 51–79. ISSN 0169-2046. https://doi.org/10.1016/j.landurbplan.2018.08.007; Groundwork (2021). Out of bounds: Equity in access to urban nature. *groundwork.org*, May. https://www.groundwork.org.uk/wp-content/uploads/2021/05/Out-of-Bounds-equity-in-access-to-urban-nature.pdf

13 Project Drawdown (2017). Educating girls. Project Drawdown. https://drawdown.org/solutions/health-and-education

CHAPTER 9

ANIMALS

240   Why save the animals?

Most humans today live in urban environments, and our lives are very far removed from the way our ancestors lived. No longer do we need to hunt animals for food or live in fear of being killed by predators. This is a triumph for our species – and it shows in the way we've taken over the planet.

But our triumph has also meant that we've forgotten how important the entire natural system is to our survival. Nature is all about balance, and if animals start to go extinct, that balance is disrupted. When the balance of an ecosystem is disrupted, a domino effect occurs and other species become endangered as a result.

Every animal plays a crucial role in the system that makes life on Earth possible. Our modern world has forgotten our dependence on nature, and that's why we must remind ourselves as often as possible that we do need nature, and we have a duty to protect it.

241   Why bees are so important

A world without bees would be a very difficult world to live in. We have bees to thank for all the different varieties of fruits and vegetables we have, for the plants and flowers growing across our planet, and for our food system.

Bees are pollinators. They've adapted through evolution to go from plant to plant, collecting nectar, and transferring pollen between different plants to help them grow. They are essential to a stable food chain and the survival of lots of different plant species.

Because of climate change, bees are having a hard time. Weather patterns aren't as stable as bees are used to and these changing temperatures have the potential to confuse them. This means they can't do the important work they do, and their numbers are dwindling because of lack of food or because of the pesticides used in our food system.

242   How many animals go extinct every day?

It's hard for scientists to figure out how many species are being lost due to human activities, especially considering scientists still aren't sure how many species exist on the planet. Estimates on how many species go extinct every day vary and are largely based on computer modelling, which means it's hard to know exactly what the truth is.

According to one study, by 2050, if some effort is made to reduce warming, we can still expect to lose 15–37 per cent of existing species.[1] All we can be sure of is that extinction rates are high, and that less global warming will mean fewer species going extinct.

243   The impact of urbanization on animals

The number of people living in urban areas rises every year, and more people on the planet live in urban areas than rural areas. Living in a city close to other people has many benefits for humans. It provides security in the knowledge that services are nearby, opportunities for collaboration, and easy access to human benefits such as friendship and culture.

But urbanization is not good news for the wildlife for which metropolitan areas were home before we moved in. When we pave roads, we cover up soil that's home to thousands of species. When we build skyscrapers, we cut down trees that would have housed mammals and birds.

Prolonged exposure to light, noise and air pollution also affects the wildlife that has managed to stay. Some species do thrive under urbanization – for example, some birds in UK cities are flourishing because of more garden availability.

Preserving green space in cities and building green architecture are a couple of ways to protect existing wildlife in urban areas. The best we can do is to encourage our governments to put these on the agenda!

244   How to save the bees

Bee populations are dwindling for several reasons: chemical pesticide usage, air pollution, rising temperatures which change flower growth patterns, and habitat loss. Here are a few things you can do to play your part in saving them:

- Plant a bee garden. You can do this on a balcony or patio or in your garden by planting native flowers and providing a shallow water source for the bees. Try advocating for your office to do this if it has an outdoor space.

- Avoid eating commercially produced honey. Bees produce honey as food to get them through the winter, providing essential nutrients to keep the hive going. In commercial honey farms, bees are given other sweeteners, which may harm their health.

- Donate to a bee conservancy project. There are many initiatives and organizations working to protect bees, providing pollinator education and creating jobs at the same time. Supporting these organizations is a great way to be an advocate for the bees.

245   Animals are adapting their body shapes to cope with climate change

It can be easy to think of nature and animals as helpless in the face of harmful human activities, but animals are much more resilient than we might think. There's new research emerging that shows animals are actually evolving to change their body size to deal with heat more effectively.[2]

Animals that have larger appendages (such as beaks, ears and tails) tend to be better at cooling down than those with smaller appendages. Some species are literally shape-shifting these appendages, increasing their size to adapt to climate change.

Some animals will shape-shift, but some won't survive. It's up to us to minimize the damage.

246 Plant vegetation along beaches to help turtles

One sea animal that has unfortunately suffered a lot because of human activity is the sea turtle. A few years ago, a video with a turtle with a plastic straw stuck in its nose went viral, showing how devastating plastic pollution can be for animals.

Straws aren't the turtles' only problem, though. It's now been discovered that rising sea levels are affecting turtle reproduction. Turtles are born with a map of their birth location and return to that location to lay their own eggs. If tides have changed, the map can become distorted and the nest area can even become submerged in water. Temperature also affects the sex of the turtles: hotter nests equal more female turtles.

What we can do to help these turtles is to plant vegetation (preferably native species) along beaches. This can provide protection for turtles on their way to the ocean and cool down and stabilize the sand. If there's a turtle beach near you, why not host a beach planting initiative?

247 How reducing car use helps animals in your area

We already know that cars aren't great for the environment. With fossil fuel-powered cars, there's air pollution and emissions. With electric cars, there are the ethical implications of the materials used to build the car. However, there's another consequence of our love of cars that is directly killing animals and their homes: road building.

Roads often get built straight through irreplaceable habitats, displacing already vulnerable species that must now navigate surviving next to busy roads.

It's a cycle: if more of us drive, the government will build more roads, which means more of us will drive, which means more roads. If governments redirected funds for road building towards investing in public transportation and improving biking and walking infrastructure, it would be much better for animals and the planet.

The government will do this if (1) we pressure them to do it, or (2) we don't drive as much. How about a healthy mix of both?

248   Why polar bears are affected so much by climate change

Until recently, the narrative and education around the climate crisis was centred on polar bears. Environmental messaging would often take the form of slogans like 'Save the polar bears' or 'Polar bears are going extinct' and global warming was talked about as if it were a future problem, someone else's to solve. Polar bears were at the centre of this conversation because, over millennia, they have been able to adapt to the Arctic habitat only.

One of the more effective and sobering ways to see climate change happening in real time is by looking at Arctic sea ice: over the past 30 years, the oldest and thickest ice in the Arctic has declined by 95 per cent.[3] If Arctic sea ice melts away completely, polar bears will lose their only home, and will have virtually no chance of surviving anywhere else, outside a zoo.

Declining sea ice means less food for the bears, which need the ice to capture their food. This decreased food energy will cause polar bears to starve, which means declining populations, which means existing bears have to go further to find a mate, which means they'll need more food energy, which isn't readily available ... The cycle continues this way until the species becomes extinct in the wild.

249 Buy sustainable paper and wood to save forest animals

Traditional paper comes from wood pulp which is made by cutting down trees. Considering that it often takes decades for a tree to grow, and we use so much paper on a daily basis, it's hard to imagine that we have any trees left at all.

We're not only cutting down the planet's best carbon sinks, we're also destroying the habitats of forest animals that live in the trees or use them as protection from predators.

The best way to save these trees from being cut down is to stop using paper altogether, use recycled paper, or buy Forest Stewardship Council (FSC – https://fsc.org/en)-certified paper, which makes sure forests are managed in a sustainable way.

250 Which animals will survive catastrophic climate change?

Climate change spells bad news for most animals on the planet, including humans (why are we doing this to ourselves?). But there are some animals that will survive the scorching heatwaves and powerful floods to come.

Any animal that reproduces quickly (unlike humans or other large mammals) is likely to avoid extinction. Scientists have also found that older species, like cockroaches, are more likely to survive than species that have evolved more recently.

Animals that have a broad range in their diet are more likely to avoid extinction too, as they can switch easily to other foods if one is affected because of climate change. Any plant that already lives in extreme environments such as a very wet rainforest or very dry desert is also likely to survive the climate crisis.

The deep sea will probably be mostly untouched by climate change, too, thanks to its vast distance from the surface, where most of the changes will be happening.

Essentially, an organism that is biologically able to adapt to extreme differences in food sources, heat and rain will probably survive the apocalypse. Let's hope it doesn't come to that.

251 Ditch lawns and plant wild gardens instead for wildlife

Beautifully manicured lawns are pleasing to the eye, but ecologically they're useless. Not only does mowing a lawn use fossil fuels, but it turns out that lawns are very water thirsty.

In the United States, the Environmental Protection Agency estimates that around a third of all public water is used to water grass.[4] When you consider that lawns aren't biodiverse and provide almost no benefit to local wildlife, the resources used to upkeep them seem very wasteful.

If you have a lawn, consider planting a mini meadow or a wild garden instead. You can do this by setting aside a patch of grass (or the whole lawn) and letting it grow. You'll be rewarded with wildflowers, and plenty of insects and healthy soil for the rest of your plants. To control unwanted plants, hand-weed as often as needed.

You can also buy wildflowers or plant native plants to help the process along. Your garden won't be as neat, but it will be a sanctuary and haven for wildlife.

252   How conservation corridors help animals

Different animals need different conditions to survive based on their evolution – some need cold and wet environments, while some thrive in dry and hot conditions.

There have always been variations in climate and weather on the planet, but climate change is making these variations more extreme and unpredictable. This is tough for species that have evolved to survive under certain conditions. To survive, these animals will need to move to other areas that suit their biology.

Around half of Earth's terrestrial surface is still untouched by humans,[5] but there are still animal species that live alongside or near human areas. If these animals want to move habitats, they might have to cross motorways, roads and fields or go around cities and towns. These obstacles severely limit their chances of relocating successfully, which is where conservation corridors come in.

Conservation corridors create 'ecological connectivity', which allows for animals to move around different habitats freely without being interrupted by human development. This is what humans living side by side with nature looks like – it means we can still develop our human societies while allowing nature to thrive.

253   Factory farms: an unnecessary evil

The first step to a just and equitable food system is to shut down factory farms. Picture thousands of chickens crammed into a small indoor space, or cows unable to move from their assigned space – this is what a factory farm usually looks like.

Factory farms are designed to churn out as much animal product as possible for the cheapest cost, regardless of the effect on the animals and the environment.

The priority of factory farms is to keep producing meat and animal products as cheaply as possible, and to increase production as the years go on. Not only will this spell disaster for the planet, but it will also subject billions more animals to cruelty and suffering.

Factory farms need to become a relic of the past, and that will happen if demand for meat and animal products decreases. Governments also need to invest in making nutritious plant-based meals more accessible and affordable, and enforce farming regulations to curb harm to the environment.

254 Birds and skyscrapers

All animals have a basic need for shelter, but we humans have really taken this to another level. We've created buildings for many different uses: homes, offices, shops, hospitals. We've also built structures whose purpose goes beyond shelter and into the realm of art – the Empire State Building, the Burj Khalifa, the Shanghai Tower.

These structures are awe-inspiring, but for birds they're often a death sentence. Anywhere from 100 million to 1 billion birds are killed every year in the United States alone due to building collisions.[6] Birds will see a tree or the sky in the reflection of a building, and fly straight into it, unaware.

Some cities have responded by turning off the lights at night during peak migration season, and legislation is being enacted to enforce bird-friendly architecture. We can only hope for more of these initiatives, as some bird species are becoming endangered because of this problem.

255 Advocate beyond your home to reduce light pollution

Even if you try as hard as you can to reduce light pollution in your home, there are still thousands of streetlights and other sources of light pollution in the city or town you live in. Light pollution is harmful for local wildlife, it's shown to disrupt human circadian rhythms, and it obstructs our view of the beautiful night sky.

Reducing light pollution in cities has surprisingly few hurdles – the main obstacle is awareness and motivation.

To help, you can join or support a local dark sky initiative. These organizations do an amazing job of raising awareness and advocating for protecting animals' right to darkness. You can also write to a local representative about banning upward-facing billboard floodlights, enforcing shades that point down on streetlights (i.e. away from the sky) and reducing lighting on beaches and rural areas.

256 Does veganism help the environment?

The world's biggest meat producers are banking on meat consumption growing over the next few years. If this happens, it will be impossible to curb climate change. A report from Greenpeace has found that the global average meat consumption per person needs to fall to around 22 kilograms (48 lb) per year by 2030, and then to 16 kilograms (25 lb) per person in 2050 to avoid the worst effects of climate change.[7]

Currently, global per capita meat consumption is at 43 kilograms (95 lb) per person, and this is projected to rise.[8]

Veganism does help the environment because it reduces the demand for meat. The government can also reduce the price of plant-based foods, which can make buying meat products less attractive as well as provide incentives for animal product farmers to switch to growing plant foods.

257   Build a birdhouse to help your local birds

Writing to your representative, getting out into the streets and protesting, supporting activists and Indigenous peoples – these are all important actions to take. But it can also be really rewarding and impactful to act on a smaller scale.

Making a birdhouse is a great way to help local birds by giving them shelter and a safe place to create a nest. It can also protect them from the elements and give them a place to stay warm in the winter.

Birds are important pollinators, and their numbers are dwindling, especially in urban areas. Their habitats are being destroyed, and extreme weather threatens their survival.

You can use materials like parts of old fences or drawers to create your birdhouse, keeping in mind that the size of the round opening will determine which kinds of birds make it their home. Be patient: it may take a while for bird visitors to arrive.

Often, when we take smaller actions to help, we're more motivated because we can see the positive impact of our actions quite quickly. This can give you the energy and positive momentum you need to take on more difficult activism.

258   Reduce light pollution at your home at night

For millions of years, animal species on this planet have adapted to the continual cycle of day turning into night, and night turning into day again. It was simple: day was light and night was dark. But in the human age, night isn't dark anymore. Night is lit up by millions of artificial lights, and this light pollution is interfering with nature.

Light pollution can disrupt animals' breeding and migratory instincts. For example, sea turtle hatchlings usually wait until night-time to emerge from their nests. Brightly lit beachfronts will sometimes confuse these hatchlings and cause them to wander inland instead of towards the shore.

City lights are the main culprit, but there are some actions we can take ourselves that will benefit local wildlife in our area. At home, try turning off any unnecessary outdoor lighting, or installing sensor-activated lighting.

A nice side effect to less light pollution is a better view of stars in the night sky. Stargazing and protecting nature – what's not to like?

259   Try not to clean up your garden too much

Everyone loves a neat garden, but too much neatness does more harm than good to local wildlife. Fallen leaves, dead flowers and rotting twigs and branches can provide protection and shelter for birds and bees during colder months. Leave this natural detritus on the ground: as they rot, they will provide essential nutrients for wildlife and soils.

Now you have an excuse to put off cleaning up the garden. Saving the planet is the perfect reason.

260   The impacts of the leather industry

Leather is an ancient fabric used by humans for thousands of years, but what used to be a necessity for warmth and protection has become a multibillion-dollar industry that is seriously bad for the planet.

Because leather is essentially treated cow skin, leather products contribute to deforestation, high water usage and methane pollution.

To process leather and stop it from decomposing, manufacturers will use tanning liquor made from a toxic chemical called chromium. In many places, the chemical-laden wastewater produced from this process is not properly managed and ends up contaminating soil or local rivers.

There are many other plant-based alternatives to opt for instead, like leather made from cork, recycled rubber or even pineapple leaves.

261   What does 'free range' mean?

If you've ever felt confused by the labelling on egg cartons, you're not alone. It can be difficult to decipher whether animals are treated well based on vague jargon such as 'free range', but let's break this term down a bit.

In essence, 'free range' means animals can be outside for at least some of the time they're reared for their meat, milk or eggs. The length of time they're allowed outside, and the space they have to roam, differ according to country regulations. In the European Union and the United States, animals must have continuous access to the open air.

The rules are vague and leave much room for interpretation for farmers, so you can never be fully sure animals are treated well. In any case, laying hundreds of eggs is stressful for chickens, and free-range cows have the same climate impact as factory cows, so free range is not necessarily a better choice.

262   How many species are endangered?

Humans are just one species, but we've had a huge impact on the millions of other species that live on Earth. An endangered species is one whose population has decreased by more than 50 per cent over the past ten years, or whose prevalence in a geographic area is less than 5,000 square kilometres (1930 square miles).

Almost every species that is endangered today is in that predicament because of human activities.

Owing to pollution, disease, habitat destruction, hunting, and pesticide usage, the number of endangered species has rapidly increased in the past 100 years.

Around 16,000 plant and animal species are currently endangered, according to the International Union for Conservation of Nature (www.iucn.org).

263 Support (monetarily or otherwise) a national park in your country

A great way to make an immediate impact towards preserving nature and wildlife habitats is to support a national park in your country. National parks play a huge role in conserving biodiversity and protecting natural ecosystems from urban development.

They are also crucial to improving scientific knowledge because there's a wealth of information that can be collected and passed on to researchers who want to understand natural systems and climate change.

It's also important to read up on the history of your national park to understand and acknowledge the people who may have lived on the land before.

Some national parks, particularly in the United States and Canada, belonged to Indigenous peoples who were forcibly and often violently removed from their homes. Today, Indigenous peoples in Botswana and India are facing violence and eviction from reserves and parks which are their ancestral homes.

If you can, support Indigenous peoples who are already conserving and protecting land. And of course, if your national park or reserve doesn't have a troubling or negative relationship with Indigenous peoples, then consider donating your money or time to it.

264   How elephants help climate change

African forest elephants that live mostly in Central Africa used to number over 1 million.

Deforestation and poaching have decimated this elephant population, and the species is now almost extinct. These elephants are different from the savanna, or bush, elephants we might normally picture on the African continent – they're smaller and their tusks point downwards.

But what's even more interesting is that these elephants fight climate change.[9]

Because they live in rainforests, they feed on young and thin trees that might compete with other trees for sunlight. The trees left behind have much better access to rain and light from the Sun, which means they grow larger than they would have otherwise. Because of their large size, these trees capture an enormous amount of carbon.

Through this process of eating thinner trees and helping the bigger trees grow bigger still, it's estimated that each African forest elephant contributes to capturing over 6,000 metric tonnes of carbon dioxide per square kilometre (17,000 tn per square mile). That's the same as the emissions that would come from driving 2,000 cars for one year!

Forest elephants often live in countries that have high national debt. To encourage these countries to protect the elephants, some UN programmes are offering to help get the debts wiped out in exchange for the elephants' protection. Deforestation in these countries is also usually high because it provides a source of income.

Stories like the carbon-capturing African forest elephant show why it's so important that we put economic value on preserving nature as a society.

265 'Adopt' a large animal

Large animals are indispensable to the planet, but they're at a higher risk of extinction because of large-scale hunting, habitat loss and climate change. This makes sense – big animals are easier to spot, and they need more energy and food than smaller animals.

Large animals eat larger volumes of food, which means their poo is typically bigger, too. This makes them soil health superheroes, because they can deposit a large volume of nutrients into the soil and increase its fertility. If we lose large animals, soils could collapse and our ecosystems and food chains would not be far behind.

There's a lot we can do at a systemic level to help stop the extinction of large animals, but if you're looking for something easy and impactful to do now, consider 'adopting' a large animal.

You can do a quick search online to find an organization that facilitates adoptions of tigers, elephants, pandas and other large animals. These organizations often use the funds from adoption to protect animals from poaching or to buy important equipment for people protecting the animals on the ground.

266 Always keep your distance

Humans have already disrupted so many of the planet's ecosystems, but there is evidence that we are also profoundly changing animal behaviours simply by our presence.

Research has found that the presence of humans can reduce the survival probability of a species or alter animal behaviours even over quite large distances.[10] For example, large birds like eagles can be affected at a distance of 400 metres (440 yd), and large mammals such as deer or elk can be affected up to 1,000 metres (1,090 yd) away.

While being outdoors is regenerative and nurturing for humans, we should be mindful of how our presence may impact the life of a wild animal. Keep your distance and respect the delicate balance of nature.

267　Pets contribute to emissions, too

Pets are essential family members – they provide us with unconditional love and contribute to our empathy for nature and understanding of animals.

When you're enjoying their love, it can be easy to forget that the food and toys we buy for them also contribute to the warming of the planet. We usually give our cats and dogs commercially made food made from meat and fish, which has a huge environmental impact. We also give them toys that are often made from plastic and require energy to produce.

While I'm not suggesting you get rid of your pet, there are some ways to reduce your pet's impact on the environment.

You can get creative and make toys for your pets with your own materials, or buy sustainable or second-hand toys in good condition.

With regards to food, try to avoid high-end pet food that uses human-grade meat. This is much worse for the environment than regular pet food which uses meat scraps.

You can also skip the beef entirely and incorporate insect-based, chicken-based or vegan pet food, both of which have lower impacts on the planet.

268 Animals and nature are the original recyclers

We have a lot to learn from animals and the resourceful ways they use what's available to them in their environment to build and survive.

Octopuses are super-smart animals and will use discarded items like coconut shells and even glass jars on the ocean floor to build shelters. Dung beetles will repurpose waste from other animals as homes or nests to lay their eggs in. Dung beetles even save the US cattle industry over $380 million a year by repurposing livestock manure.[11]

There is no waste in nature – everything that exists has been made from something else, which will die and become something else. But most of the products humans make create waste that is a dead end. Waste is an industrial and human and capitalist design error. Recycling and circular design are everywhere in nature because it's the most efficient and smartest way to create things. We must remind ourselves that nature already has all the solutions. This is a profound realization, and reminding ourselves of this fact is another way to increase our ecological empathy.

269 How whales cool the planet (so don't eat them!)

Whales are incredible stores of carbon, and they are essential to the oceans' health and the entire planet's ecosystem.

The main benefit of whales to the planet comes from their huge size. When whales dive towards the bottom of the sea, their huge body mass pushes water towards the ocean floor, which disturbs nutrients and makes them go from the bottom of the ocean towards the surface.

This process feeds marine plants that do the important job of absorbing carbon and giving us oxygen. Something as simple as a whale diving gives us more oxygen.

A whale's body also accumulates carbon over its long life, and when it dies, that carbon is stored inside its body at the bottom of the ocean.

Upsettingly, there are 90 per cent fewer whales today than there have been for thousands of years. The blue whale is even rarer – the population has shrunk by some 99 per cent since 1900 owing to the activity of the whaling industry.[12] We must protect whales by supporting their conservation, fighting for their protection to be put into law, and avoiding eating them.

References

1   Thomas, C. D., Cameron, A., Green, R. E. et al. (2004). Extinction risk from climate change, *Nature*, *427*(6970): 145–148. ISSN 0028-0836

2   Ryding, S., et al. (2021). Shape-shifting: Changing animal morphologies as a response to climatic warming. *Trends in Ecology & Evolution*, *36*(11): 1036–1048.

3   Osborne, E., Richter-Menge, J., & Jeffries, M. (2018). Effects of persistent Arctic warming continue to mount. *Arctic Report Card: Update for 2018*, 3 December.

4   EPA (2017). *Outdoor water use in the US*. WaterSense: An EPA Partnership Program, 19 January.

5   Jacobson, A. P., Riggio, J., Tait, A. M., and Baillie, J. E. M. (2019). Global areas of low human impact ('Low impact areas') and fragmentation of the natural world. *Sci. Rep.*, 9(14179). https://doi.org/10.1038/s41598-019-50558-6

6   Loss, S. R., Will, T., Loss, S. S., & Marra, P. P. (2014). Bird-building collisions in the United States: Estimates of annual mortality and species vulnerability. *The Condor*, *116*(1): 8–23. https://doi.org/10.1650/CONDOR-13-090.1

7   Tirado, R., Thompson, K. F., Miller, K. A., & Johnston, P. (2018). *Less is more: Reducing meat and dairy for a healthier life and planet – Scientific background on the Greenpeace vision of the meat and dairy system towards 2050.* Greenpeace Research Laboratories Technical Report (Review), March 2018.

8   Ritchie, H., and Roser, M. (2017). Meat and dairy production. Published online at https://ourworldindata.org/meat-production Retrieved from: https://ourworldindata.org/meat-production [Online Resource].

9   Chami, R., Cosimano, T., Fullenkamp, C., & Oztosun, S. (2019). Nature's solution to climate change. *Finance and Development, 56*(4): 34–38.

10   Dertien, J. S., Larson, C. L., & Reed, S. E. (2021). Recreation effects on wildlife: A review of potential quantitative thresholds. *Nature Conservation*, 44: 51–68. https://doi.org/10.3897/natureconservation.44.63270

11   Losey, J. E., & Vaughan, M. (2006). The economic value of ecological services provided by insects. *BioScience, 56*(4): 311–323. https://doi.org/10.1641/0006-3568(2006)56[311:TEVOES]2.0.CO;2

12   Roman, J., Estes, J. A., Morissette, L., Smith, C., Costa, D., McCarthy, J., Nation, J., Nicol, S., Pershing, A., & Smetacek, V. (2014). Whales as marine ecosystem engineers. *Frontiers in Ecology and the Environment, 12*: 377–385. https://doi.org/10.1890/130220

CHAPTER 10

MONEY AND FINANCE

270   Start impact investing

Making money and making the world a better place at the same time is called impact investing. The basic idea is that you can invest your money into a market that needs capital to work on the world's most pressing problems.

The key to being an impact investor is having the intention to have a positive impact through your investments. This is different from someone who just happens to invest in renewable energy. For the impact investor, if social or environmental goals are furthered, then that investment is deemed a success.

The assumption of the impact investor is that if the capital is being used to improve the world, then it's likely there will be a financial return.

This type of investing is quite new, but it's growing in popularity, and it's a great way to have a positive impact whilst growing your money.

271   Does your bank support fossil fuels?

From 2015 to 2020, the world's 60 biggest banks invested $3.8 trillion in fossil fuels.[1] When we hold money in a bank, some portion of that money goes into a fund that's invested by the bank.

As consumers of the bank's services, we don't have a choice where that money goes. This means it's very likely that your money could be funding deforestation or coal production without you even knowing it.

If you do a quick search online, you can investigate your bank to find out what they're investing your money in. The best way to act against this is to switch banks and voice your concerns to your bank.

If they know customers are switching because of climate concerns, they're more likely to cut down on harmful investments.

272   Switch to a green bank

So you've just found out your bank invests in fossil fuels. When you've recovered from the initial shock, it's time to find a new bank that will invest your money ethically.

Green banks don't usually stop at investing your money ethically. They can also buy climate offsets to become net zero or even net positive, which means they 'remove' enough or even more carbon from the atmosphere to cover their daily operations. Some green banks also have lending programmes, offering loans to individuals or companies to buy electric cars or invest in solar panels.

Deciding who to entrust with your hard-earned money isn't easy. You may need to read the fine print to make sure you're making the right choice.

273   How banks are contributing to climate change

Imagine you're an oil executive and you've been tasked with securing funding for a big project drilling in the North Sea.

Drilling for oil and gas is an expensive business – you might need to hire thousands of engineers, sending them to live (all expenses paid) on an oil rig for months on end, and you'll need to power massive drills and pumps *and* transport the extracted resources safely.

Without funding, oil and gas companies would not be able to get all of this done. As the oil executive, it's your job to go to a bank and convince them this is a worthwhile investment.

Because of the way our economic system works, the only incentive for banks is the return on their investment. They're not required (by law) to consider the impact of their investment on the planet.

This is how banks have contributed to climate change. For decades, they have been funnelling money into oil and gas projects and collecting the returns. More money means more oil and gas drilling. More oil and gas drilling means climate change.

274   Is cryptocurrency bad for the planet?

Cryptocurrencies are digital currencies that are alternatives to money issued by governments. As the popularity of cryptocurrency increases, concerns have been raised about the enormous amount of energy digital 'mining' requires.

Cryptocurrency uses blockchain technology and relies on 'mining' to create new coins and make sure the network is secure. Mining involves complex mathematical calculations that require specialized computers.

Miners receive Bitcoin or other cryptocurrencies as a reward for verifying transactions, because they keep the cryptocurrency secure. These rewards incentivize miners to connect lots of computers and servers so they can keep mining – a process that needs a lot of electricity. The currency is then tracked on the blockchain, which is the equivalent of a bank's balance sheet. This process also requires considerable energy to maintain.

However, energy use and emissions aren't necessary linked. It all depends on how the energy is created. If the energy used for powering cryptocurrencies is renewable, then the emissions created by mining cryptocurrency can be low. Some cryptocurrencies are also moving towards other mechanisms for rewarding miners that are much less energy intensive (such as proof of stake).

There are some cryptocurrencies, like BitGreen, which are eco-friendly alternatives to Bitcoin, rewarding miners both for verifying transactions and for taking eco-friendly actions.

Almost every type of human activity on the planet releases emissions, including fiat money (legal tender paper or coin money), because our system and global economy are reliant on fossil fuels to keep them running. As cryptocurrency enters the mainstream and becomes more regulated, governments may offer incentives for miners to use renewable energy, and more environmentally friendly low-power coins could be created.

However, if there's anything the cryptocurrency debate teaches us, it's that the world desperately needs to transition to renewable energy, and fast.

275   Will carbon taxes save the planet?

Being able to eat meat for every meal or fly on a plane have long been considered luxuries. But in the Global North these activities have become so popular and commonplace that we seem to be prepared to rapidly heat the planet so we can carry on doing them.

A carbon tax is a possible solution to this problem – the government could add a tax onto the price of carbon-intensive activities to account for the cost of doing the activity to the planet. The basic idea is that if it's more expensive to fly, fewer people will so, and carbon emissions will be reduced.

The carbon tax idea sounds good in theory. But a carbon tax on everyday activities could end up making inequalities worse because the burden of the tax will be much higher on lower-income individuals. It could also shift the blame of climate change away from the institutions and companies that caused the climate crisis in the first place.

The oil industry received $11 million worth of subsidies every minute in 2020.[2] We're definitely better off turning off that tap first, investing that money into a green transition, and then deciding if implementing a carbon tax is necessary.

One way to equitably implement a carbon tax is to return the collected revenues from carbon taxes to the poorest in society in the form of a tax cut or a 'carbon dividend'.

276   The effects of cash on the planet

Did you know that the U.S. Mint loses money every time it produces a cent coin?[3]

The sourcing and mining of raw materials like copper and zinc, along with production and transportation, mean that making a one-cent coin costs approximately 1.43 cents.

In 2014, the US Mint used 510 tonnes (562 tn) of copper and 19,857 tonnes or 21,888 tons of zinc to make 8.1 billion one-cent coins. The same year, in the United States, 81 tonnes (89 tn) of copper was used to make other consumer products, appliances, ammunition and electronics.[4]

It's not easy to mine copper ore – and it costs the planet more than a pretty penny. Small coins like the cent or penny are also not currently recycled by many governments.

Banknotes aren't much better. They are usually made from either paper that gets soiled easily and so have to be replaced often, or from polymer (i.e. plastic).

As you can see, there's no easy solution to making cash green – other than going cashless, of course. Countries including Canada, Australia, Brazil and Norway have now stopped producing their smallest-denomination coin. We'll see if others follow suit.

277   Why are sustainable products more expensive?

Sustainable products are often associated with luxury, but buying products that haven't harmed people or planet during production shouldn't be a luxury.

Unfortunately, in a capitalist system, economic profit is the only measure of success for a business. This means that business owners have an incentive to reduce the cost of their products so they can make more money, and don't have an incentive to consider the environment or ethics.

Usually, reducing the cost of a product can be achieved by making more of it and taking advantage of discounts that come with bulk production. However, most companies have chosen the route of increasing efficiency at a cost to our planet and the people making their products. For example, fast-fashion companies want the cheapest materials to create clothes, like cotton grown with pesticides or fossil fuel-based polyester.

Materials that are good for the planet take more time, effort and care to produce. Products that have been made by people that are paid well cost more. Instead of trying to make everything cheaper, we should be changing the system to make sure everyone can afford sustainable goods.

278 Do we have enough money to fix climate change?

A common argument by climate deniers is that climate change is too expensive to prioritize.

According to the World Bank, the world will need to invest $90 trillion in infrastructure by 2030 to transition to a green economy.[5] That sounds like a lot, but what's often overlooked is that $1 invested in the green transition will return $4 in value to the global economy.

We can also most certainly afford it. For comparison, the world spent almost $2 trillion on military and defence in 2020 alone.[6]

We desperately need more investment in renewable energy and sustainable infrastructure, but there is currently too little investment happening too slowly. More government money is being spent on fossil fuels than renewables, and many countries can't afford to make a green transition.

The countries that can afford to invest in a green transition should be leading the charge and helping others to adapt. That's not happening.

The more important question is can we afford not to fix climate change? Absolutely not.

279   Why aren't governments spending more to fix climate change?

The climate crisis is happening now and it's already taking lives and displacing people from their homes. It's not an exaggeration to say that every year that we keep pumping carbon dioxide into the atmosphere, we sign more and more death sentences.

Climate change threatens to destabilize the global economy and cause a worldwide health crisis. Air pollution already kills more than 7 million people every year. So why aren't governments treating this like the crisis it is?

The key problem is that our entire global economic system heavily relies on fossil fuels and profit making. Those who are most vulnerable to the effects of climate change have little power against wealthy elites who profit from fossil fuel exploration and extraction. Powerful fossil fuel lobbies spend millions every year to stall government action on climate change. And it's working.

To fix climate change, we need to change our economic system and take power away from those who profit from the burning of fossil fuels. It's not going to be easy, but there's a lot of power in unity. If you're reading this, you're already part of the change.

280   How much money is wasted when we waste food?

If you've read Chapter 4: Food, you'll already know that food waste is a huge problem for the planet. But did you know that the monetary value of global food waste is estimated at $1 trillion?[7]

The United States leads the world in throwing away food: approximately half of all produce.[8] Despite the enormous amount of food waste, one in eight households in the United States is food insecure, which means they don't have access to enough affordable, nutritious food.[9]

Most food waste happens at the farm or supermarket level – crops can be ruined, produce can be thrown away for cosmetic reasons, and edible parts of food can be thrown away during manufacturing.

There is a huge economic upside to saving food from going to waste, enough to encourage governments, businesses or even you, dear reader, to come up with solutions.

281   Is living sustainably more expensive?

Sustainable living is perceived as more expensive, which discourages many people from making sustainable lifestyle changes. Indeed, sustainably made products are usually higher quality and built to last, so they come with a higher price tag than mass-produced products.

These high prices for sustainable goods mean sustainability is usually perceived as inaccessible. But we must differentiate between how sustainability is marketed to us versus what sustainability actually is.

Sustainability is marketed as expensive recycled swimwear, special bamboo food containers or fancy food waste apps. In reality, living sustainably is mostly about reducing waste and overconsumption.

For example, by making sure you eat all the food in your refrigerator, you're living sustainably. By reusing the plastic containers you already have, you're living sustainably. By renting clothing for a special occasion, instead of buying an item and never wearing it again, you're living sustainably. By voting for politicians who prioritize climate change, you're living sustainably.

These actions are easy and inexpensive. It's enough to simply survive, and do our best to try to change the exploitative system we live in.

282   Is sustainability a luxury?

Sustainable products are made to last because they use high-quality materials and they are usually made by someone highly skilled and well paid.

If we define luxury as something in short supply and of the highest quality, then sustainability *is* a luxury. But for us to continue living on this planet, we will need another definition for luxury.

Luxury is currently about exclusivity and status and sending messages to others about who we are based on what we buy. Sustainability is about making and buying products that we can continue to make and buy for a long time without sacrificing the future of life on this planet. Sustainable products today are luxurious status symbols, and this needs to change if we want to have any hope of saving the planet.

If everyone can't buy sustainable products, then how can we hope to solve the climate crisis? We can make sustainable products cheaper, which they will be if more people buy them. We can also make everyone on the planet a bit richer so they can afford sustainable products in the first place.

283   If you can afford it, buy an electric car to make it cheaper for everyone else

Buying a fossil fuel-powered car today is generally perceived to be more affordable than buying an electric car. Electric vehicles use newer technology, which can be more expensive. But electric vehicles are better for the environment and human health, so government support in the form of subsidies and tax breaks is available, which can bring down the price significantly.

Demand is growing for electric cars, which means companies are incentivized to produce more, which can lower the price even more over time.

Electric cars are more expensive than petrol or diesel-powered cars but have comparatively lower running costs.

If you can afford to buy an electric car now, and you want to do your bit to increase demand (and therefore decrease the price) for these cars, go ahead!

284   Should billionaires be 'donating' to climate change?

After Jeff Bezos's trip to space, which released millions of ozone-damaging particles into the atmosphere, he made a $1 billion donation to conservation projects, on the grounds that 'Earth looks fragile from space'. Similarly, Bill Gates pledged $1.5 billion to combat climate change on the condition that the US government passed a $1.2 trillion infrastructure bill. The two richest people on Earth are spending more money on climate mitigation than entire governments.

Bezos said that going to space changed his perspective of the world, that from space the atmosphere seemed 'thin' and 'fragile'. So shouldn't we be happy that we have the richest man in the world on our side? Not necessarily. Because the donations are private, it's very difficult to know what exactly the funds from these donations will be used for and if they will be spent well.

Indigenous groups have said for decades that money invested in conservation often goes towards paying consultants who 'teach' Indigenous peoples how to conserve. The irony is that Indigenous peoples already have a wealth of knowledge on conservation and have been preserving and protecting biodiversity better than any other group.

Action: If you have the means, try donating to Indigenous conservation groups to support their efforts directly.

285 Who profits from climate change?

It's practically guaranteed that the whole world will have to deal with some level of climate change, but there are some companies and countries that are trying to profit from the effects.

The Netherlands has dealt with its fair share of flooding in the past few years, and some Dutch engineers are selling their flood-management knowledge to other countries that will need to tackle sea level rises.

There are also reports of investors from the United States, Saudi Arabia and China buying up farmland in anticipation of a poor economic future. Agricultural land that provides commodities and has access to water is a stable investment and could bring substantial profits if other farms' crops fail due to climate change.

If you're interested in this topic, consider reading McKenzie Funk's book *Windfall: The Booming Business of Global Warming* (Penguin, 2014).

286 Can you buy your way to sustainability?

We've been told for decades that sustainability is a consumer choice, that if we care about the planet we need to buy only sustainable products. But can we buy our way to being sustainable?

Imagine for a second that you're rich and live an unsustainable lifestyle – you use your private jet to go on vacation, eat a lot of steak and caviar, and you buy new clothes every week. You wake up one day and decide you want to spend as much money as necessary to be sustainable.

You'd invest in an electric car, transfer your investment portfolio to focus on green companies, put solar panels on the roof of your mansion, and buy enough offsets to cover your yearly released emissions. These are all incredible actions to take, and sure, your personal contribution to climate change would decrease. But it wouldn't stop climate change.

We can't buy our way to being sustainable. We need to change the system that allows climate change to happen in the first place – and that's done by voting, by organizing and advocating for those who will be affected the most by climate change, and by spreading the word.

287 How to prepare your investment portfolio for climate change

If climate change is going to be solved, any solutions will need plenty of investment, and will probably have huge upsides for investors if they end up being implemented.

Renewable energy is going to be a huge part of the energy mix in the future if we want to keep living on this planet. So any investments in this area, especially solar, are probably a smart bet.

Green technology such as electric cars, sustainable construction materials, meat substitutes and carbon capture are also promising possibilities to look at for your portfolio.

Any industry that might be affected by natural disasters, such as real estate or insurance, could be risky investments.

288 How your pension could be saving the planet

If you're putting away money towards a pension, you probably want to make sure the human species won't be extinct by the time you're old enough to cash it out. One of the best ways to ensure that future is to make sure your pension isn't being invested in projects that might assure our extinction.

Transitioning your pension pot so that it gets invested in green and sustainable projects is estimated to be many times more powerful than giving up flying and eating plant-based combined.

If you've been meaning to make the switch and haven't done so already, this is your sign!

289 An economic system that could save the planet

Our current economic system is based on extracting value from people, animals and planet to make a profit, without considering the consequences to natural systems. The system also allows a handful of people and countries to hoard wealth, creating inequality which has catastrophic effects on human society.

Some economists advocate for 'degrowth' as a solution to climate change, arguing that chasing economic growth for growth's sake will destroy the planet. But degrowth is an unpopular idea in developing countries especially, which often rely on economic growth to alleviate poverty.

Doughnut economics is an economic theory written about by Kate Raworth in her book *Doughnut Economics: Seven Ways to Think Like a 21st-Century Economist* (Cornerstone 2017). The model gets its name from the doughnut shape in which the outer ring represents the ecological ceiling we must not cross if we want to continue living on the planet. The inner ring represents basic human rights, and the 'dough' is the ideal prosperity for humanity in which all needs are met while respecting planetary boundaries.

This is a very interesting concept that could solve many of the problems we face today such as poverty, lack of housing and education, and fair access to water, food and healthcare. If we grow just enough to be in the 'dough', humanity can prosper without destroying the planet in the process.

290   How to go green on a budget

Being sustainable doesn't have to be expensive. The best way to go green is simply to consume less and make use of what you already have. You don't need fancy sustainable products to lead a sustainable lifestyle, despite what some advertising wants you to believe.

With clothing and furniture, buying second-hand is both cheaper and better for the environment.

Instead of buying disposable products, try to invest in products you can reuse. For example, use cloth towels instead of paper towels, and safety razors instead of plastic ones. By doing this, you can save money in the long run and save single-use plastic from going to landfill.

Eating a plant-based diet can also often be cheaper than eating a meat-based diet, depending on where you live and the convenience you need.

A great sustainable and money-saving hack is to go grocery shopping later on in the day when some items have reductions on price. These are often thrown out if not bought, so you can snag a discount *and* save food from being wasted.

291   What are carbon credits?

Some industries and companies have products or manufacturing operations where emissions are unavoidable, and carbon credits are a possible solution to this.

Carbon credits are like 'permission slips' that can be bought by companies to allow them to emit a certain amount of carbon dioxide. This gives companies an incentive to lower their carbon emissions so they can avoid paying for carbon credits. The money from carbon credits usually supports conservation and ecosystem protection.

Most developed countries already have some form of a carbon credit in place right now. Critics of carbon credits argue that they can give companies free rein to pollute, and contribute to slowing down systemic changes. But supporters say they provide essential funds to developing countries to help them protect ecosystems and adapt to climate change.

292   Support regenerative agriculture with your money!

Farmland is very expensive and farm real-estate prices have doubled in the last decade.[10] Regenerative agriculture – the future of food and farming – requires long-term thinking, so can be a struggle for farmers trying to make ends meet and afford to pay rent on expensive land.

BIPOC farmers in the United States are also more likely to be tenants than owners of land,[11] and receive less funding and support than their white counterparts.[12] Funding for farmers can give them the incentive and support they need to switch to regenerative methods.

Farmland is also becoming an attractive investment for impact investors who want to encourage regenerative farming and support farmers, while achieving long-term financial returns. While this is an area that's usually restricted to accredited investors, there are some organizations that allow anyone to participate monetarily or otherwise to support regenerative farmers. Slow Money (https://slowmoney.org) is an organization to check out if you're interested.

293   When companies commit to 'net zero', what does that mean?

'We're company x, and we're committing to net-zero emissions by 2050.' You've probably seen this (or a variation of this) statement released by many different companies over the past few years. Releasing PR statements like this means the company has made a pledge to 'balance' its emissions by removing or reducing them.

However, these pledges are often nothing more than PR statements that give us a false sense of security that the company cares and wants to take action. The key is in the deadline – 2050 is too far away for pledges to make any measurable difference to the climate crisis now.

In 2021, the planet was about 1.09 degrees Celsius warmer than preindustrial times. If we want to avoid the very worst of climate change, we need to keep warming to below 1.5 degrees. We'll likely reach this temperature much sooner than 2050, which makes company 'net zero by 2050' pledges remarkably inadequate.

294   Donate to adaptation projects if you want to make the biggest impact

Climate change is already here, and it's already affecting the lives of the poor and vulnerable around the world. 'Adaptation finance' is becoming a popular philanthropic and investment tool to help communities adapt to climate change.

Climate adaptation is about minimizing harm and making the best of a bad situation.

Adaptation finance also includes supporting the most vulnerable populations (such as Indigenous peoples, farmers, women) to increase their resilience. These populations' voices must be heard and brought centre-stage so that adaptation projects can help them effectively.

Adaptation projects can include flood management solutions, upgrading infrastructure to be more resilient against natural disasters, improving food security and protecting forests.

If you want to help those who are already dealing with the effects of climate change, consider donating to adaptation projects that centre on the voices and needs of the most vulnerable.

295   To what extent do governments subsidize fossil fuels?

Governments actively spend money to reduce the cost of fossil fuels and increase our dependence on them at a time when we should be rapidly transitioning to renewable energy. Subsidies make fossil fuel products cheaper and more accessible. This can be important for people on lower incomes. However, cheap fossil fuels drive demand for products made from fossil fuels, which actively destroy the planet and air quality.

According to an analysis by the International Monetary Fund, global subsidies in 2020 were estimated at about $6 trillion, with China, the United States, Russia, India and Japan responsible for two-thirds of subsidies.

Reducing subsidies would make renewable energy cheaper and more accessible, and this would cut emissions.

296 How to know whether a company is *really* green

It can be difficult to cut through green jargon and buzzwords to understand whether a company is really as sustainable as it says it is.

Whether you're choosing to buy from a company, work at a company, or invest in one, it's important to be able to recognize whether it is truly aligned with your values.

Oil companies, in particular, are guilty of using words like 'net zero' and 'tackling climate change' on their websites while still pursuing new oil and gas drilling. As consumers, we need to be able to tell which companies are talking the talk versus walking the walk.

To spot this, watch out for big, general claims without evidence or hard numbers to back them up. There's currently no law against misleading sustainability claims – something that needs to change – so keep this in mind the next time you go to vote. It should not be the responsibility of the consumer to sift through greenwashing jargon to make a responsible choice.

Any company that's truly pursuing environmental change will be able to give you more detailed information if you reach out and ask for it. If they can't provide any more details, or if they claim to simply buy offsets instead of making tangible changes to their business, then you'll have your answer.

297   A template to send to your bank to encourage them to divest from fossil fuels

Want to do a quick good deed for the planet? Here's a template of a letter/email to send to your bank to urge them to divest from fossil fuels:

> Dear [Bank Name],
>
> I've been a customer with your bank for x years and I'm writing to inform you of my decision to move my business to a bank that is better aligned with my values. I believe it is your institution's moral responsibility to make sure your customers' funds are not used to finance the fossil-fuel industry.
>
> Climate change is a direct threat to the future of life on this planet, and the fossil-fuel industry is culpable for crimes against nature and humanity. Fossil-fuel companies have pushed an agenda of misinformation and have delayed climate action for the sake of their own profits.
>
> I urge you to reconsider your investment in fossil fuels and join the thousands of institutions which have divested and made a commitment to ensuring a safe and healthy planet for future generations.
>
> Yours sincerely,
>
> [Your Name]

298   What is an ESG fund?

When you're an investor, it can be challenging and time consuming to understand whether a company truly has a positive effect on the environment. ESG funds are a solution to this problem.

ESG stands for environmental, social and governance, and an ESG fund is a portfolio of different companies that have been especially chosen because they meet rigorous ESG standards.

Sustainable investments and ESG funds are set to thrive in the future and will benefit from the inevitable green transition we'll need to make. Markets may be quite volatile in the meantime, because of the uncertainty around climate change, so invest in ESG funds at your own risk and with the longer term in mind!

299   Who will pay for the green transition?

The world will need to spend money to avert climate change's worst consequences, but who exactly is going to shell out the cash?

Governments and intergovernmental organizations like the United Nations are going to be the biggest investors in a green future. It is their responsibility to enact policies that will discourage corporations and consumers from harmful spending, and help the world transition to a green economy smoothly.

Corporations are the next biggest spenders on the list. The biggest emitters will have the responsibility of both reducing their emissions and increasing their investments in climate finance.

Sadly, the companies that contribute the most emissions have the most to gain from the status quo, which is why fossil-fuel companies spend so much money lobbying to delay climate action. Corporations will ultimately respond to consumer pressure, and there is already evidence of this working.

The other actors who will pay for a green transition are private investors, banks and individual consumers who all have a role to play in assisting and encouraging the green transition on a smaller but no less important scale.

References

1   Rainforest Action Network, et al. (2021). *Banking on climate chaos: Fossil fuel finance report 2021.* https://reclaimfinance.org/site/en/2021/03/24/baking-climate-chaos-fossil-fuel-finance-report-2021/#iLightbox[gallery10024]/0

2   Parry, I., Black, S., & Vernon, N. (2021). Still not getting energy prices right: A global and country update of fossil fuel subsidies, IMF Working Paper WP/21/236. International Monetary Fund.

3   USM (2014). Production and sales figures. United States Mint.

4   CDA (2017). Copper supply and consumption, 1996–2016, annual data. Copper Development Association.

5   The New Climate Economy (2018). *The 2018 report of the Global Commission on the Economy and Climate.* https://newclimateeconomy.report/2018

6   SIPRI Military Expenditure Database (2021). https://doi.org/10.55163/JTFI7245

7   Hetrick, S. (2017). Wasted food is wasted money. Sustainability Accounting Standards Board, 19 March.

8   Gunders, D. (2017). Wasted: How America is losing up to 40 percent of its food from farm to fork to landfill. Natural Resources Defense Council. Retrieved from https://www.nrdc.org/sites/default/files/wasted-2017-report.pdf

9   Coleman-Jensen, A., Rabbitt, M. P., Gregory, C. A., & Singh, A., *Household food security in the United States in 2019*, ERR-275. U.S. Department of Agriculture, Economic Research Service.

10 Rippon-Butler, H. *Land policy: Towards a more equitable farming future.* National Young Farmers Coalition. https://www.youngfarmers.org/land/wp-content/uploads/2020/11/LandPolicyReport.pdf

11 Horst, M., & Marion, A. (2019). Racial, ethnic and gender inequities in farmland ownership and farming in the U.S. *Agriculture and Human Values, 36*: 1–16. https://doi.org/10.1007/s10460-018-9883-3

12 Cowan, T., and Feder, J. (2013). *The Pigford Cases: USDA Settlement of Discrimination Suits by Black Farmers*, Washington, DC: Congressional Research Service. https://nationalaglawcenter.org/wp-content/uploads/assets/crs/RS20430.pdf

CHAPTER 11

WORK

300   The impact of full email inboxes

If you needed another excuse to clean up your email inbox, here's a kicker. Did you know that unread emails and full email inboxes contribute to climate change? As long as the world keeps being powered by fossil fuels, everything we do will have an impact on the climate, and emails are no exception.

Emails require energy to store and send information, and all email activities are powered by servers which need electricity to keep running. The more emails we send and store and leave unread, the more electricity gets used to run the servers.

This isn't to say you should never use email again – after all, sending an email is much less energy intensive than sending a letter. But this can serve as a reminder to be mindful of our society's reliance on fossil fuels. Emails are mundane and normal, but they still contribute to the climate crisis. Let's change that!

301   How to talk about climate change in the office

The office is often apolitical, and since climate change is so heavily politicized, it can be tricky to navigate raising awareness about it in an office setting. But we need to start thinking of offices as what they really are: humans gathered together, working on a shared mission.

Climate change is affecting and will affect all humans, including the office and the world of work. Once we start to think of climate change in this way, it can be easier to start a conversation that might otherwise be 'too political'.

The office is a great place to start if you want to raise awareness about climate change. I recommend starting a sustainability committee and gathering everyone interested in these issues in one place. It can be easier to raise awareness about something if you have the support of a few people already. As a group, you can plan events or talks to engage your co-workers in conversations about climate change.

Offices contribute to climate change and will be affected by climate change. We need climate leadership in offices in every industry. All it takes is someone to start the conversation, and that someone could be you.

302   Can companies help the planet?

We spend most of our lives at work. This means employees have a lot of power to take action to reduce the emissions associated with work. We often look towards governments to make change, but companies can also make sustainable changes that align with both the planet and their business.

Companies can offer remote work and provide incentives and benefits for employees to encourage them to use public transportation or cycle to work. Offices can use recycled or compostable products for printer paper and paper towels and use green cleaning products. To go a step further, companies can join programmes like 1% for the Planet (www.onepercentfortheplanet.org) and dedicate a portion of profits to organizations that do important climate work.

We need everyone in the fight to save the planet, powerful corporations included. There are exceptions to this, however.

Some companies have business models that depend on exploiting the planet, people and animals for profit. Unless these organizations completely overhaul their businesses, it's unlikely that buying a few offsets or providing recycled printer paper will help. That's why system change is so important.

303   The powerful lobbying of Big Oil

As I was writing this, the biggest climate action event in history took place in Glasgow: the 2021 United Nations Climate Change Conference, or

COP26. The purpose of the conference was to bring the world together to make pledges to tackle climate change.

There were 503 fossil-fuel lobbyists at COP26, which was more than the number of delegates from any nation, including the United States. The fossil fuel industry was better represented at the conference than the combined representation from eight countries that have felt the worst effects of the climate crisis – Myanmar, Puerto Rico and the Philippines among them.

The fossil-fuel industry caused climate change, and there is evidence that they should have known the damage their industry would have on the planet as far back as the 1960s.[1] Powerful lobbying in the decades since has been targeted towards discrediting climate scientists and delaying climate action in politics.

To this day, the five largest oil and gas companies spend almost $200 million a year lobbying with the effect of delaying or blocking climate action.[2] They are one of the biggest obstacles to fixing climate change.

304   The four-day work week

The five-day work week has been the norm since the 1920s, but does it make any sense that the average person today is working like a factory worker did 100 years ago? There are some who advocate for a four-day work week as a way to reduce emissions, increase happiness and improve quality of life.

Commuting, heating office buildings, powering electronics and video calls all require energy, so switching to a four-day work week could reduce energy usage.

There are also studies that show a four-day work week has no effect on productivity and helps workers feel more fulfilled in their careers. Research estimates that a four-day work week would reduce the UK's carbon footprint by around 20 per cent.[3]

With so much technological advancement, and automation replacing plenty of human jobs, a four-day work week could be easily implemented.

305   Will we need a universal basic income?

The way our economy works now is destroying the planet. Endless economic growth and consumption is not possible on a finite planet with finite resources.

That's why, in an effort to find a better system, some have advocated for a universal basic income as a way to support economic growth while sustaining a high quality of life for all. A universal basic income could be implemented by unconditionally giving a set amount of money, say $1,000, to every person in a country. This would be financed by taxing things that are less dependent on economic growth – such as inheritance, land or assets.

A universal basic income could increase worker negotiating power, provide freedom to individuals stuck in abusive situations, and increase happiness. There are even theories that implementing a universal basic income could solve overconsumption because people would have more time to do things they really loved and wouldn't need to turn to consumption as a short-term fix or distraction.

Productivity has never been so high, but workers haven't been seeing these increases reflected in their wages.

A universal basic income can fix this problem and can also allow us to be human again, to spend time in nature or with loved ones, or do hobbies we love, if we so choose.

306   The benefits of more office greenery

If you needed even more evidence that humans really need nature, consider that studies have shown greenery in offices significantly improves worker satisfaction and concentration.

Just looking at greenery can improve our mental health and reduce stress.

Simply adding plants to an office space has been found to increase productivity by 15 per cent.[4] Nature is so important, so let's integrate it into our lives where we can, starting with the office.

307   How heat will impact the workplace

As the atmosphere fills with carbon dioxide and the planet warms, extreme heat will become more frequent.

Our bodies are designed to work effectively at room temperature, so the more we experience extreme temperatures, the less effectively our bodies and brains are able to function.

Anyone who works outdoors or in non-air-conditioned spaces will be at a high risk of experiencing heat stroke, dehydration or accidents. Extreme heat will affect poorer people in lower-income countries the worst, including farmers, construction workers, garbage collectors and other essential workers.

Although 90 per cent of US households have air conditioning, only 8 per cent of people living in Africa, Asia, Latin America and the Middle East have air conditioning.[5] This means that even those who work indoors in these countries could be most affected.

308   Start a rooftop garden in your office

There are so many benefits to surrounding ourselves with greenery, especially in an office space. Rooftop gardens can provide employees with a green escape, improving productivity and mental health and reducing stress. They can also help reduce energy costs for the building, contribute to cooling on hot days, and cater to local wildlife.

There are some companies that will install and maintain a rooftop garden for an office, but it's easy for office managers to do this themselves. Just get hold of some pots, soil and seeds and get planting!

Starting an office garden is also a great way to engage employees and build community in the office.

309   Green jobs are on the rise

Thinking of a career change? Your job could save the planet. Here are some of the careers that are going to be in demand as the world gears up for a green transition:

- *Urban farmers.* People who grow food in urban settings such as rooftops.
- *Solar photovoltaic installers.* People tasked with assembling and maintaining solar panel power-generation systems.
- *Wind turbine specialists.* Wind energy use is going to increase tenfold, so wind turbines will need lots of technicians to oversee them.
- *Green home builders.* Experts in transforming existing buildings and homes to make them more sustainable.
- *Green designers.* Architects and landscapers who can design buildings to be more environmentally friendly.
- *Sustainability consultants.* Consultants who help companies implement green strategies and practices.
- *Environmental scientists.* Scientists who specialize in identifying and preventing threats to the environment.

310   How climate change will change the way we work

We have all witnessed how disruptive a global pandemic can be to work, but climate change is going to be a different ball game.

Climate change will cause uncertainty about the future, which will change pension and retirement planning. Extreme changes in weather will change the construction industry. Concerns about sustainability will transform the fashion industry.

The way we adjust to climate change will truly be unprecedented: no one in history has ever had to adapt to changes on a planetary scale.

Employees and managers in the future will all need to have a basic grasp of climate change, in much the same way that we're now expected to have a grasp of computers and the Internet.

Engineers will have to get used to more volatile weather patterns when planning construction, big fashion executives will need to consider the effects of extreme heat on garment worker productivity, and delivery companies will have to help their drivers adjust to new laws around zero-emission cars.

No industry is safe from the climate crisis, but it will be interesting to see the innovations that come from this shift.

311   Turn off idle electricity in the office

All too often, computers are left plugged in over the weekend, office lighting is left on overnight, and radiators heat empty meeting rooms over Christmas. Leaving electronics and lighting on when they're not in use wastes a significant amount of energy and contributes to global warming. Leaving lighting on overnight for the average office wastes enough energy to heat water for 1,000 cups of tea.

Installing automated lighting is one of the easiest ways to save money on idle lighting costs and save energy in the process.

Unplugging idle equipment such as computers, monitors, printers and dishwashers at the end of the workday or week can also save a substantial amount of energy.

312 Consider your commute

Remote working and commuting have changed irreversibly because of the COVID-19 pandemic, with more people working from home than ever. This has significantly affected emissions, because commuting involves travel, and travel usually produces carbon emissions.

If you're not already working from home, a challenge for you is to switch up the way you commute if you can. If you usually drive, try out a different way of getting to work. Carpooling, public transportation or cycling are all great options that can expose you to different experiences and maybe even new people.

This challenge will not only help you get out of your comfort zone but make you more aware of the infrastructure in your local area. This will empower you to be a more informed climate voter – maybe your town needs more bike lanes or more investment in public transportation.

313 Instate an electronic recycling or donation programme for the office

Most of the carbon emissions involved in producing an iPhone come from the initial production process. Around 20 per cent of the emissions come from transporting the iPhone from the factory to the shelf.[6]

This is the case for most electronics, which means that if we recycle and refurbish our electronic items, we can save a lot of the emissions associated with their initial production.

Electronic waste, or e-waste, is everywhere, and it's estimated to reach 74 million tonnes (82 million tn) per year by 2030.[7] E-waste releases toxic substances like mercury if not disposed of properly.

That's why it's very important for businesses to recycle old electronics and not simply throw electronics away. Electronic recycling programmes pick up wires, plugs, laptops, computers, monitors and other electronic equipment to be repurposed and given a new life.

314   What kind of electricity powers your workplace?

If you've ever walked through the office district of your city, you'll notice that office buildings are huge. They're designed to supply electricity, lighting and heating to thousands of people at a time, and this energy needs to be uninterrupted and reliable. Because these buildings are so huge, the energy costs can be astronomical. But they don't have to be.

If your office building's energy is being supplied by fossil fuels, it may be time to consider switching to a renewable energy supplier. The energy is just as reliable, because green suppliers have a diverse range of energy sources to pull from. The energy can often be cheaper, too, especially when gas prices are high. Saving the planet often involves saving money, too.

That's my favourite kind of win-win, and probably your office's, too.

315   Take inventory of your workplace greenhouse gas emissions

If you want to understand how much of an impact your office has on the planet, it can be useful to take inventory of where your office's emissions are coming from. Knowledge is power, especially when it comes to understanding which changes can have the most impact on the planet.

You can do this by sending an employee survey asking how people commute, measuring how often employees take business trips, or what kind of energy is used to heat and cool your office buildings.

Taking inventory can help you identify which areas need improvement and can also raise awareness of the issues surrounding climate change among employees.

316 Increased carbon in the air will affect our decision making

There are endless articles online that give advice on how to make the best managerial decisions, and productivity apps that promise to increase our work output. It turns out, though, that the increased carbon dioxide in the atmosphere may be thwarting our efforts to stay productive.

A study conducted for the journal *Environmental Health Perspectives* found that workers exposed to higher levels of carbon dioxide in the office showed shortcomings in decision making.[8]

Even though climate change is affecting the outside world, it's slowly creeping into our indoor lives. Carbon dioxide build-up in the atmosphere could directly affect businesses by hitting their employees' brain functions. So why aren't they doing more about it?

317 Skip the paper towels in the office

Before paper towels became so widely used in office toilets, the cloth towel was the norm.

The US inventor of the paper towel, Arthur Hoyt Scott, had trouble selling his invention until he rebranded it as 'more sanitary' than a cloth towel. He advertised them as single use, which limited the spread of germs.

However, the way we use paper towels today is more about convenience than sanitation. Paper towels have now become a way to dry clean hands in office toilets, multiple times a day.

To produce paper towels, we need to cut down trees. The more we refrain (as hygienically as possible) from using paper towels, the more trees we can save.

Personally, I'm partial to the air-drying technique – I let my hands dangle and slightly swing by my sides and they're usually dry within a couple of minutes.

318   Cut down on unnecessary emails

Email is such a huge part of modern life – and it doesn't seem to be going away any time soon. Most of us take for granted how much electricity is needed to power our everyday activities, and since we don't see the equipment that powers our emails, it's easy to assume it doesn't need much electricity.

Every time we send an email, electricity is used to power the computer that does the sending, the server that receives and sends the email, and the router that enables the wireless sending.

The problem is that most electricity is generated by burning fossil fuels. Alongside advocating for more renewable energy usage, we can also be more mindful of how much of our email emissions can be reduced.

Action: Try to avoid sending unnecessary emails, emails with very large attachments, or with lots of recipients.

319   Take the stairs!

If you're able-bodied, taking the stairs instead of the lift/elevator can be a great way to conserve energy and move your body while you're at it.

Every time we use a lift, we use electricity. Until our energy grids are 100 per cent renewable, every effort we can make to reduce the amount of fossil fuels burned for electricity is a win for the planet.

320   Do we really need so much paper?

Watch an episode of the US TV series *The Office* and you'll be forgiven for thinking the paper industry is dying a slow death. In reality, paper and cardboard production worldwide is actually increasing every year.[9] The world's biggest consumer of paper is China, followed by the United States and Japan.

Our paper addiction hasn't stopped, although most of the growth is attributed to cardboard for packaging. But we should still be mindful of our paper consumption.

Paper and cardboard make up 20 per cent of global waste, but they're also the easiest items to recycle. All we need to do is adjust our relationship with paper so we consume only what we need.

321   Organize a climate 'lunch and learn' in your office

There's nothing like breaking up a workday with a 'lunch and learn' event to learn something new. Organizing a lunch and learn with someone in the climate space can be a great way to conduct climate leadership in your office and raise awareness in the process.

Lunch and learns can foster teamwork and team bonding in a low-pressure setting and can also be a springboard to making wider sustainable changes at the company. Plus, everyone loves a bit of free food.

322   Create a green office committee

A green committee at work can be an impactful way to make a difference and meet with other people who care about the planet as much as you do. Community and collaboration are powerful tools to make change because we certainly can't save the planet all on our own.

A green team can track company sustainable goals, make suggestions to management for sustainable change, engage employees to take action in their own lives, or organize events like park clean-ups.

The most successful green teams assign specific roles, meet regularly, and invest in climate education for employees and management. It's really what you make it, so set some goals and have fun with it!

323 Consider subsidizing public transportation options

Aside from easing employee commuter costs, offering public transport benefits is a great way to take part in reducing emissions as a company. Companies can offer discounted or free seasonal tickets or offer an interest-free loan to employees to purchase one.

Using public transport is one of the most environmentally friendly ways to travel. Companies can do a lot to encourage planet-friendly behaviours where they can.

324 Bring your own lunch to work!

It's handy that making green changes can be beneficial to our wallets, too. Packing your own lunch to take to work is much more cost-effective than buying lunch, not to mention much more sustainable.

A takeout lunch often comes with disposable cutlery and packaging, which creates unnecessary waste. We're all human, though, so if you have a hankering for a ready-made lunch, try to support your local small food businesses if you can.

325   Have your company partner with green non-profits

One of the best ways a business can make an impact is through partnering with green charities or non-profits. Businesses are powerful, and often it takes just one company speaking out on a certain issue to change entire industries.

In 2020, 42 big businesses (including Amazon, IBM, General Motors) partnered with the Center for Climate and Energy Solutions (www.c2es. org) to push government to pass climate policies. Their joint statement said that company policies must 'meet the needs of marginalized communities, low-income households, and workers and communities disadvantaged by the energy transition'.

This is important because it draws attention and urgency to the issue of climate change. However, partnering with a non-profit organization is not a replacement for doing the work to reduce businesses' impact on the planet and the marginalized.

Partnering with an environmental non-profit can also take the form of raising funds for green causes, providing training opportunities for employees, or investing in innovative green solutions for your business.

326   Give office furniture a second home

If your office has furniture or IT equipment that's no longer in use, consider donating these items to local charities or schools.

Furniture is bulky and difficult to recycle, and it often ends up in landfill. Donating these items can help non-profit organizations focus on doing the important work and save furniture from going to landfill in the process.

There are plenty of organizations that handle the donation process, or you can reach out to local charities directly to donate.

327   Support your local economy with office events

The next time your office has an event, consider buying food and other items directly from small businesses in your local area. Supporting a small business is beneficial for your community, because such businesses are more likely to support local causes or employ local people than big businesses.

Small businesses also have a lower environmental impact because they're more likely to source their products locally and getting their products to your event won't require shipping.

Running a small business takes so much dedication that advertising and marketing sometimes become an afterthought. Supporting your local economy by using small businesses for these events can give them some much-needed exposure and word-of-mouth.

328   Do we really need office swag?

We all love free stuff, but is it worth spending money and planet resources on a company T-shirt most people will just wear in bed? Probably not.

The most environmentally friendly option for swag is to avoid giving it out at all, but you could provide eco-friendly items if management insists on it. Some ideas for eco-friendly swag are reusable coffee cups with your company logo on them or a reusable water bottle made from recycled materials.

Swag doesn't build employee engagement or loyalty as much as team building does. It can be much more impactful to invest in a memorable experience for employees instead of an item.

329   Give employees volunteer days

It's becoming increasingly harder to retain employees with traditional office perks like free food and fancy offices. Giving employees volunteer days can give your company an edge and improve workplace satisfaction all at once.

Volunteer time off gives employees the opportunity to give back to their community without having to sacrifice pay. This is becoming a popular benefit as businesses can see the value of investing in a meaningful and fulfilling experience for employees.

Not only is this rewarding for everyone involved, but it can encourage people to volunteer who may not have considered volunteering otherwise. Giving employees volunteer days can also boost retention, foster teamwork and bonding, and improve employee soft skills.

A great example of a company that does volunteer days well is the US software company Salesforce, which gives employees up to seven paid days to volunteer, and top volunteers are given prize money to donate to a chosen charity.

References

1   Robinson, E., & Robbins, R. C. (1968). *Sources, abundance, and fate of gaseous atmospheric pollutants*. Final report and supplement. United States.

2   InfluenceMap (2019). *Big Oil's real agenda on climate change: An influence map report.*
https://influencemap.org/report/How-Big-Oil-Continues-to-Oppose-the-Paris-Agreement-38212275958aa21196dae3b76220bddc, March 2019

3   Mompelat, L. (2021). Stop the clock: The environmental benefits of a short working week. *Platform*, May.

4   Nieuwenhuis, M., Knight, C., Postmes, T., & Haslam, S. A. (2014). The relative benefits of green versus lean office space: Three field experiments, *Journal of Experimental Psychology: Applied*, *20*(3): 199–214. https://doi.org/10.1037/xap0000024, 2014

5   IEA (2020). Is cooling the future of heating? IEA. https://www.iea.org/commentaries/is-cooling-the-future-of-heating

6   Apple (2021). Product environmental report iPhone 13. https://www.apple.com/environment/pdf/products/iphone/iPhone_13_PER_Sept2021.pdf, 14 September.

7   Forti, V., Balde, C. P., Kuehr, R., and Garam, B. (2020). *The Global E-waste Monitor 2020: Quantities, flows and the circular economy potential.* United Nations University/United Nations Institute for Training and Research, International Telecommunication Union, and International Solid Waste Association.

8   Allen, J. G., MacNaughton, P., Satish, U., Santanam, S., Vallarino, J., and Spengler, J. D. (2016). Associations of cognitive function scores with carbon dioxide, ventilation, and volatile organic compound exposures in office workers: A controlled exposure study of green and conventional office environments. *Environmental Health Perspectives, 124*: 805–812. http://dx.doi.org/10.1289/ehp.1510037

9   Berg, P., and Lingqvist, O. (2019). Pulp, paper, and packaging in the next decade: Transformational change. *McKinsey*, 7 August. https://www.mckinsey.com/industries/paper-forest-products-and-packaging/our-insights/pulp-paper-and-packaging-in-the-next-decade-transformational-change

CHAPTER 12

PLANTS

330 Which plants are the best at absorbing carbon?

We know that plants need carbon dioxide to survive and grow. It takes around six molecules of carbon dioxide to make one molecule of glucose for every single plant. If the plant grows faster, it'll absorb more carbon than a slower-growing plant.

This is good for the short term, but fast-growing plants tend to decompose easily or not live as long. When a plant dies and decomposes, it releases all the carbon it has stored over its lifetime.

One of the best ways to clean up the atmosphere is to plant a variety of plants that have different benefits to the planet. Hardwood trees like oak and beech are great for storing carbon over a long period of time, while fast-growing plants like hemp and bamboo are great for absorbing carbon fast.

You can use this knowledge when thinking about what to plant in your own garden or home. The more plants we have on the planet, the more carbon is absorbed, so don't hold back!

Try to plant trees like hazel or blackthorn, which may fit better in the average garden than a bigger tree like oak. Supplement that with other shrubs and native plants and the planet and local wildlife will thank you.

331 Why is biodiversity important?

Climate activists and conservation groups talk about biodiversity a lot – but what is it and why is it important?

Biodiversity is the variety of different plants, animals, fungi, bacteria, insects and microorganisms living in an environment or habitat, and the greater the variety, the healthier the ecosystem. This is because each organism in the ecosystem has evolved to play a specific role, each providing some benefit to the life around them.

In a nutshell, biodiversity supports life on Earth. Without it, life would cease to exist. Biodiversity provides us with food, helps stave away sickness and disease, gives us a diverse range of nutrients necessary for survival, filters our air and water, and much more.

Greater biodiversity means more protection against disease and natural disasters because if one species is affected by a disease or pest, there are plenty of others to take its place.

By encouraging nature and wildlife in wilderness, rural and urban areas, and protecting existing wildlife, we can preserve biodiversity. We should also support Indigenous peoples, who currently protect up to 80 per cent of biodiversity on the planet.[1]

332 Can soil save the planet?

Soil is more than just dirt that feeds our plants. It's one of the biggest carbon sinks we have on the planet, and the healthier it is, the more effective it is at storing carbon. When plants grow in soil, they extract carbon dioxide from the atmosphere and store that carbon in the soil. If soil is unhealthy or degraded, it releases stored carbon back into the atmosphere.

Healthy soil also provides habitats for different insects and fungi, which are essential to life on Earth and to making sure our food chain doesn't collapse.

Over 30 per cent of the planet's soil is degraded because of deforestation, monoculture farming (when only one type of crop is grown, reducing biodiversity), pollution, wildfires and urbanization.[2] Healthy soil is easily lost, but difficult to gain back, as it can take decades to build.

Action: Start cultivating healthy soil in your own garden by composting, avoiding the use of peat, and allowing a little natural 'mess' with rotting wood and fruit. Whatever you can do to improve your soils and increase biodiversity is great for the planet.

333   Why community gardens are important

Picture this: it's a Saturday afternoon and you're thinking of places in your local area to hang out and pass the time.

If you live in an urban area (which over half of all humans do), then your options for activities are probably to go to a restaurant, a cinema or a museum or go shopping. These activities require money to take part in. There are very few places left that we can enjoy for free – green spaces and libraries are two examples.

Community gardens are an emerging way to engage with nature, grow fresh food, learn new skills, and connect and share with others – without needing to spend money.

Check if there's a community garden near you, and if you have the time, start one! Community gardens can improve food security in a community, reduce food emissions, and provide much-needed greenery in urban areas.

If you plan to start one, check with your local government about empty or unused allotments, and try to engage local groups like schools or businesses to take part.

334   Plant conservation needs more attention

Conservation means to prevent the loss of something.

In the context of the climate crisis, conservation means minimizing the deaths of animal and plant species that can't survive a warmer and more dangerous world.

More plant species than animal species go extinct every year, but plants don't get the same PR animals get. It's harder for us to relate to plants than to other animals because we're animals ourselves. Around two in five plant species are now threatened with extinction,[3] and this is bad news because we rely on plants for medicine, food, energy and clean air.

There are many examples of conservation movements that have worked, and without which we would have lost species for ever (bald eagles, songbirds).

The best ways for you to contribute to plant conservation are to spread awareness and to support your local botanical garden. Botanical gardens are doing essential work to support threatened plant species and are often the only places a given plant species can thrive.

335 How does photosynthesis work?

You may remember learning about photosynthesis at school, but let's put it in the context of climate change so we can understand how important this process is to life on our planet.

Photosynthesis is the process by which plants use light energy from the Sun to grow and survive. Plants take in carbon dioxide from the air, water from their roots, and light energy from the Sun. They use these different elements to create sugars for the plant to grow, and oxygen is released as a by-product of this process.

Photosynthesis is the reason our planet harbours life, and we can't solve the climate crisis without it.

The more carbon we pump into the atmosphere, the more we'll need plants to replace that carbon with oxygen. That means we need to do everything we can to make sure plants stay alive – by nurturing the soil they grow in, by not cutting down trees, and by planting more plants and trees everywhere we can.

336 How 'super plants' could help our fight against climate change

Plants are already our planet's superheroes, absorbing around 30 per cent of the carbon humans emit every year.[4] Even so, there's a scientist who has been at work for the past few years trying to create 'super plants' that are even better at absorbing carbon.

Dr Joanne Chory and a team of biologists at the Salk Institute for Biological Studies, San Diego, are engineering plant roots to grow bigger and deeper and to produce more suberin (a compound that's good at absorbing carbon).

Changing plant genes in this way has the potential to remove around 46 per cent of excess carbon dioxide emissions.[5]

While we shouldn't rely on carbon capture as a free ticket to emit as much as we want, Dr Chory's solution could help us avoid the worst of the climate crisis.

337   Algae: our possible secret weapon

When we picture efficient carbon absorbers, we think of rainforests like the Amazon. But there's a secret weapon hidden in the oceans that's up to 400 times more efficient than a tree at removing carbon dioxide: algae.

Algae uses photosynthesis to absorb carbon dioxide and emit oxygen in the process. Around every second oxygen molecule we breathe in is produced by algae from the ocean. Algae also grows faster than plants, covers wider areas, and could be used as a biofuel.

Researchers are only just starting to understand the power of algae, and it could end up being part of the solution to remove lots of carbon from the atmosphere.

To contribute individually to the growth of algae, consider buying algae products to support the industry, supporting political efforts to use algae, or even growing it in your backyard if you can.

338 Support rewilding at home

There's no denying that well-kept gardens and manicured lawns are beautiful to look at, but rewilding, which discourages tidiness in nature, is gaining momentum as a way to give nature a helping hand. The United Nations has said that the world must rewild and restore an area the size of China to support climate commitments.[6]

Rewilding is all about humans giving nature the necessary tools to thrive and stepping back to let nature restore itself. Leaving nature alone is key to repairing the damage we've already done to natural ecosystems. Here are some ways you can contribute to rewilding from your own home:

- Embrace the 'messy' and leave fallen debris and leaves on the ground in your garden. These items can provide essential shelter for birds, insects and bees which do such important work for the planet and our food chains.

- Understand which plants are native to your area and plant those. Native plants are important because they've evolved to specifically support the local and native ecosystem of animals and insects.

- Install a pond or a bird bath in your garden to provide refuge and a drink for local animals and pollinators.

339 Just looking at nature can benefit our mental health

If you ever feel stressed or mentally run down, looking at some greenery or nature can provide some much-needed relief. Fighting climate change and thinking about ecosystem collapse is really taxing but spending time in nature can remind us of what we're doing it all for.

The way we live in modern times is vastly different from the environments we evolved to live in. Even looking at a photograph or painting of nature can boost our mood, increase positive feelings, and give us a sense of belonging to and appreciation for the natural world.

We need nature much more than it needs us, which is why we should be fighting to preserve it.

340 How a gardening hobby can help the Earth

Thinking about biodiversity and ecosystem loss can be really draining because the problem is so large and out of most people's control. But it's important not to lose hope and not to give up on caring for our precious planet. The best places to start taking action are within your local community and immediate environment.

Gardening is one powerful way to increase resilience in your local community, especially if you plant flowers and trees that are beneficial to local wildlife. Birds, bees and other important pollinators love variety and plants that are native to their area.

Make sure not to clean up your garden too much to allow safe havens for different critters – which improves the health of your soil.

Provide little baths or ponds for local wildlife to cool down in.

It may not feel or look like much, but every action we can take to help nature survive and adapt in our local community is crucial and important to the entire planet.

341 How urban gardens can help heat islands

If you've ever been in a city in the dead of summer, you've probably experienced heat that feels suffocating and unrelenting. That's not an illusion: cities really are hotter than almost anywhere else.

Urban areas become 'heat islands' because of an abundance of dry surfaces like roofs, pavements and buildings. These surfaces trap heat from the sun and emit it back out.

Cities also tend to have limited greenery, which contributes further to a heating effect. Trees and plants emit moisture into the air and provide shade, which can cool down temperatures.

The solution to the heat island effect is to incorporate more greenery into cities. Urban gardens and green roofs are two solutions that don't require massive changes in city infrastructure and can be easily implemented. Both can use existing empty space on the roofs of office buildings or on the balconies of residential homes.

Even small green spaces in urban areas can tackle the heat island effect.[7] An experiment in Lisbon, Portugal, found that a green area of just 0.24 hectares (0.59 acres) reduced temperatures by 6.9 degrees Celsius in the neighbourhood, as compared to surrounding neighbourhoods.[8]

Some countries have tax incentives for installing green roofs, so be sure to check the regulations in your local area. You can also try to encourage the building owners of your home or office to implement greenery, which can help on a bigger scale.

342   Best plants for soil health

Soil health is essential to life on this planet by providing a home for thousands of organisms and food for every terrestrial animal. Improving soil health can help soil absorb more carbon and grow more resilient, healthier plants.

Like everything in nature, plants and soil are connected. Healthy soil grows healthier plants, but plants can also contribute to healthier soil. Let's explore what kinds of plants help enrich soil and prevent soil erosion.

One great rule of thumb is not to allow soil to be uncovered, as it can dry out and kill the organisms living inside. Cover crops are a great solution for this because they cover soil like a carpet. Clover is an easy cover crop to start with to plant in your own garden.

Dandelion is an example of a plant that's great for soil, as it accumulates and brings up nutrients from deep below the soil surface through its roots, making these nutrients available for other plants. It also helps soil aerate and reduces erosion.

Another great way to improve soil health is to provide lots of mulch. To do this, find native, fast-growing plants and bushes that you can cut up so you don't have to buy pre-packaged mulch.

343   How to cultivate ecological empathy

We already know from Chapter 1 that ecological empathy is important for saving the planet. Modern society's disconnection from nature is partly to blame for the climate crisis. If we don't understand natural systems and how fragile they are, it's much too easy to take nature for granted.

The best way to increase ecological empathy is to understand the role we play within our ecosystem and that humans are a part of and not separate from nature. Try to be in nature more often. When you're in a green space, acknowledge that you're an inextricable part of the ecosystem – affirm this to yourself. Pay attention to how you feel. Being in nature is a wonderfully healing and nurturing experience. Lean into that feeling and allow it to envelop you.

Try to increase your exposure to nature on a daily basis, in whatever way you can. For example, you can plant a garden just for fun – not for growing 'useful' things such as fruits or vegetables, but just for the sake of it. You can also learn about animal behaviour by watching nature documentaries. When you observe nature, consider how the experiences of animals and plants mirror our own, and acknowledge our similarities.

Don't be afraid to have conversations about ecological empathy with others. Every human responds positively to nature, whether we're aware of it or not, and whether the exploitative system we live in likes it or not. You can be the person to spark this awareness in others.

344   Hemp is a panacea

The word 'sustainable' is often associated with fancy futuristic tech that'll suck carbon out of the atmosphere and solve all our problems. But what if I told you there's an ancient plant that humans have used for thousands of years to solve all sorts of problems?

That plant is hemp. Hemp has had a bad reputation for about a century now because of its association with the drug cannabis (which is just another name for hemp).

After the Great Depression, the United States ramped up its cotton production, and cotton corporations together with synthetic plastic companies tried to reduce the threat hemp posed to their businesses. And a formidable threat it was. In the United States, for decades, the cultivation of all hemp, whatever it was used for, was made virtually illegal.

Hemp is one of the strongest natural fibres in the world. It has the same tensile strength as steel,[9] which makes it a great option for rope and construction materials. It makes excellent concrete, keeping interiors cool when it's hot and warm when it's cold. If it had been used as ubiquitously as cotton is today, a *lot* of water and soil would have been saved.

Hemp needs up to 80 per cent less water to grow than cotton, and it replenishes soil as it grows (whereas cotton tends to deplete soil of its nutrients). If hemp had been planted everywhere around the world – and it truly can grow anywhere – it would be absorbing up to four times more carbon than traditional forests.

It's almost painful to imagine how different the world could have been if hemp hadn't been criminalized or stigmatized – not to mention how many Black and Latinx people could have avoided excessive imprisonment.

But it's not too late – and there are various organizations and companies trying to bring this plant back into mainstream use. If you have the ability, you can support these companies and the growth of hemp.

345   How plants can reduce noise pollution

More human beings than ever are living in urban areas, and lots of humans condensed into cities makes for a lot of noise.

Noise pollution is harmful for both animals and people – it disrupts our circadian rhythms and increases stress. The constant whir of construction, beeping and engines is enough to drive someone into poor mental health.

As usual, nature has the solutions. One of the best defences against noise pollution is to plant trees and plants and to increase the number of green spaces. Plants and trees deflect and absorb sound waves, and different types of plants deflect different types of noises.

Putting plants on your windowsill or filling your balcony with greenery is a great way to reduce some of the outdoor noise coming into your home. But we should also tell our politicians to increase green space and tree planting in our local areas.

346   The power of planting trees

Trees are one of our most effective tools against carbon accumulating in the atmosphere. They also provide shelter for local animals, reduce flooding and deflect noise pollution.

If you have a garden, planting a couple of trees is a great investment to make in the planet's future as well as in your local community.

Large, slow-growing and long-lived tree species like oak and maple are the best at storing carbon dioxide, but some smaller tree options that might be better for home gardens include elder, field maple, hawthorn, holly and yew.

347 How 'gangsta gardening' changed a community

In the face of a global calamity like climate change, it can be difficult to stay hopeful or have faith that we, as individuals, can make a difference. And while it might be true that most of us can't change the world, we *do* have the power to make change in our local communities.

No one understands this better than Ron Finley, known as the 'gangsta gardener', who has transformed dozens of empty lots in Los Angeles into community gardens. He started by planting fruits and vegetables in a strip of greenery on the sidewalk outside his house, and when he was told by the city that this was illegal, he got the law changed.

The area he lives in – South Central Los Angeles – has plenty of fast-food restaurants and liquor stores, but healthy or fresh food stores are scarce (check out Chapter 4: Food for more on this).

Ron saw a problem in his community – lack of fresh and healthy produce – and used the power and skills he had to create positive change. I hope this inspires you to think about your own strengths and how you can leverage those to transform your own community for the better.

348 Biomimicry: what we can learn from nature

Biomimicry is a fancy word for 'nature knows best'. It's a process of designing solutions in architecture, infrastructure, food systems, health and urban planning that mimic nature.

The science around biomimicry is quite new. It involves studying systems that occur in nature and applying them to human activities to minimize our ecological impact. Balance and efficiency are inherent to natural systems – there is no waste in nature.

Mammals breathe out carbon dioxide, which plants use as food to produce oxygen, which mammals breathe in.

Animals eat plants, which get turned into excrement that is an excellent fertilizer for soil to grow new plants.

Honeycombs are in the shape of a hexagon, which is the most efficient way to store the most amount of honey in as little space as possible.

Scientists and designers are using nature as an example to design wind turbines arranged like schools of fish, wetsuits that mimic the skin of beavers, or temperature-controlled buildings that take inspiration from termite mounds.

I encourage you to observe examples of the design ingenuity of nature. By thinking about what we can learn from nature, rather than what we can take and exploit, we can ensure a long future of living peacefully with it.

349   How plants regulate the Earth's water cycle

Hold your hand up to your mouth and breathe as though you're trying to fog up a mirror. You probably feel a hot, slightly wet sensation on your hand. That's water vapour that was expelled by your body. Plants have a similar mechanism, and this mechanism supports life on Earth.

Plants are responsible for most of the flow of water from the land to the atmosphere. As plants grow, they absorb water through their roots from the ground, and once the plants have finished using this water, it's released to the atmosphere through tiny pores in their leaves. Because what goes up must come down, this transpired air comes back down to land as rain, giving us the water cycle.

Even though plants have been doing this for millions of years, human activity is disrupting this natural cycle. Read the next section to find out why.

350   The end of the cooling shade of a tree

If you've ever been in a greenhouse before, you'll remember the hot and sticky feeling you get when you're inside, and the relief of cooler air when you step out of it. Human activity on this planet is turning the planet into a massive greenhouse, which is not so bad for the plants, but spells trouble for humans and other animals.

As we discussed in the last section, plants release water vapour through pores in their leaves. These pores open and collect carbon dioxide molecules, but if carbon dioxide is abundant in the atmosphere, they don't need to open as wide. This means plants will release less water vapour if carbon dioxide levels are high.

This will increase the risk of drought and could make the planet feel even hotter. As plants and trees release water vapour, they have a cooling effect on the air. This cooling effect will be weaker if plants release less water, which means trees may not offer the cooling respite they do today.

Scientists aren't certain about how plants will adapt or react to higher carbon dioxide levels in the atmosphere, or how these changes will affect the water cycle.

Considering this uncertainty, our safest bet is to take emergency action to stop pumping carbon dioxide into the atmosphere, so future generations can have enough water and experience the cool shade of a tree.

351   Plant protein: the future of food?

As the population of the world grows, the question of how to feed everyone will be one of the biggest problems we'll face as a species. But it doesn't have to be.

Plant protein is quickly becoming a popular alternative for those who still want the health benefits of protein, and even the taste and texture of meat, without the negative environmental effects. Using animal agriculture to feed people is highly inefficient. The amount of land and resources needed to rear animals is astronomically high compared to plant-based foods. For example, the average water footprint per calorie for beef is 20 times larger than for cereals and starches.

So you see the problem: if we feed our growing population with beef, we'll run out of water. And what's more, we already produce enough food to feed everyone, but much of this food is either wasted or given to livestock.

Around 33 per cent of land worldwide is used to grow plants for livestock.[10] That's why plant protein is a great alternative. We're already growing plants to feed animals, why can't we just eat them ourselves?

Thankfully, the world is catching on. Grocery aisles have more plant-based 'milks', 'bacon' made from carrot skins, 'burger patties' made from soy protein, or seitan fried 'chicken'. Plant protein is the future.

352   Regenerative agriculture is the future

Humans have relied on agriculture for thousands of years, growing crops and rearing animals for food and sustaining livelihoods. But today, agriculture is big business. We now have 'factory farms' which grow crops and rear animals at huge scales to make profits.

The problem with farming on a huge scale is that it degrades soil. Growing just one type of plant in soil is called monoculture, and it reduces biodiversity and soil health.

Regenerative agriculture is the opposite of this, and it's worth noting that Indigenous communities have been practising it for generations. The Iroquois in the north-east of North America, for example, have been growing 'Three Sisters' of corn (maize), beans and squash together because these species are known to complement each other and improve soil health even more when grown together.

Regenerative agriculture is a practice that maintains or increases soil health and maximizes the water efficiency of the plants that are grown. It can also improve the carbon sequestration of soil, which is essential to combatting climate change.

Regenerative agriculture is absolutely the future of global food farming, and governments ought to be writing it into law.

353   Are rainforests like the Amazon really the 'lungs' of our planet?

We already know that trees release oxygen. That's why rainforests like the Amazon are often referred to as the lungs of the Earth. It's unsurprising, then, that deforestation and rainforest burning make for distressing news headlines. But is it fair to say that these rainforests are solely responsible for producing the oxygen we breathe?

The Amazon's net contribution of oxygen to our planet is less than you might think, 6–9 per cent.[11] There are bigger sources of oxygen than rainforests like the oceans and algae. But the Amazon is important for reasons other than producing oxygen. It's rich in biodiversity and is a vast carbon sink for the planet. Rainforests consume most of the oxygen they produce because plants use it to respire and animals living in the rainforest breathe it in.

If the Amazon rainforest was destroyed, lack of oxygen wouldn't be our biggest problem. There would be other, perhaps more devastating consequences such as mass extinction events and huge losses in biodiversity.

354   If we planted millions of trees, could we fix the climate crisis?

Trees give us oxygen and absorb carbon dioxide, so planting more and preserving the trees we already have is certainly one solution to the climate crisis. However, preserving nature for the sake of saving the planet is incompatible with the way our global economy works. In the context of capitalism, trees are nothing more than resources that represent monetary value. Capitalism does not reward us for saving trees; it rewards us for cutting them down.

We're losing approximately 15 billion trees a year.[12] If we had started decades ago, planting trees would have been a great solution to climate change. But trees take at least ten years to start absorbing carbon. Forests have to be maintained for at least a century to be effective carbon stores. If they're cut down, the stored carbon is released.

The entire world would need to plant trees on a huge scale and pledge to maintain forests for over a century. Like almost anything related to climate change, things are not as simple as planting a few trees and hoping for the best. That's why it's so important that we change the way we value nature.

355   What are the most bee-friendly plants?

Bees are essential workers. Just one bee can pollinate thousands of flowers in a day. These tiny creatures are the reason we have so many fruits and vegetables to eat because their pollination supports food production around the world.

If you read No. 244 in Chapter 9: Animals, you'll know why it's so important to make sure we support bees, and how human activity is significantly decreasing bee populations. Bees have evolved in line with the Earth's changing seasons, but the seasons change more erratically with climate change.

If you want to do your part, you can set up a nectar oasis for bees by planting their favourite flowers in your garden or on your balcony. In the summer, bees love sweet-smelling lavender and hawthorn bushes. In the spring, they love apple trees, bee balm and chive flowers.

If you want an easy potted plant to grow that you can also eat, try planting some mint or chives and harvesting only half, leaving the rest to flower for the bees.

356   Enjoy nature, but stick to the path

We've already talked about why getting out in nature is so important – we can cultivate ecological empathy, improve our mental health, and feel a sense of oneness and belonging with the planet. To enjoy nature, you can spend hot summer days at the beach, cold winter days playing in the snow, or mild days going hiking in forests and national parks.

In every situation, however, it's important to stick to the paths which have been set aside by professionals as appropriate for humans to explore. Sticking to paths protects nature and minimizes disruption to natural ecosystems. Stepping off trails can expose plant species and soil to trampling, from which it can take hundreds of years for nature to recover.

Beaches, in particular, are important habitats for all sorts of marine animals, and human disruption can disturb or even harm these animals.

It can be so tempting to go off the beaten track to explore something new – it's human nature to be curious and a tad rebellious.

But if we want future generations to be able to enjoy nature, we need to stick to the path.

357 How the houseplant industry is impacting the planet

The houseplant industry has exploded over the past decade, which is understandable because plants are beautiful and calming and beneficial for human health, but this industry can be problematic for the environment.

Companies which sell houseplants pre-grow the plants in peat, which looks a bit like soil but is formed from partially decayed organic matter. Peatlands absorb carbon extremely well, and harvesting peat to grow houseplants in it releases huge amounts of stored carbon. Peat is a non-renewable resource because it forms very slowly.

There are more peat-free options available, so switch if you can. If your local plant shop or business doesn't have peat-free options, express your concerns about peat. You never know, they might start providing peat-free options because someone asked.

358 The dangers of chemical pesticides

Even though pesticides make life easier for growers, they're not friends to the environment. Pesticides are designed to kill a certain pest, but they can easily make their way into other areas of the environment and cause destruction.

Pesticide residue on plants may kill wildlife or cause it to avoid the food it needs and starve. Chemicals from pesticides also find their way into water and soil and can potentially disrupt entire ecosystems. If we want to stand a chance in our struggle against climate change, we need healthy soils and oceans, which are both important stores of carbon.

If you have a garden, try to opt for natural pesticides. If it's accessible to you, buying organic food can send a signal to the food industry that there is demand for pesticide-free produce.

Otherwise, as always, vote for politicians who care about reducing pesticides in agriculture, and support organizations that advocate for organic and regenerative farming.

359 Choose native plants for your garden

Planting species that are native to your area is a great way to support your local ecosystem and nurture your soil.

Native plants have adapted and evolved to a specific area over a long period of time and are depended upon by the local animals that evolved alongside them. Native plants require less maintenance and less water than foreign plants that haven't adapted to live in certain ecosystems. By choosing to plant native, you are creating a healthier, more robust environment for local wildlife to adapt to climate change.

Your own garden is a great place to start making a difference, but policymakers and city planners should also prioritize planting native plants.

References

1   Sobrevila, C. (2008). *The role of indigenous peoples in biodiversity conservation: The natural but often forgotten partners.* World Bank.

2   Arsenault, C. (2014). Only 60 years of farming left if soil degradation continues. *Scientific American*, 5 December. https://www.scientificamerican.com/article/only-60-years-of-farming-left-if-soil-degradation-continues/

3   Lughadha, E. N., et al. (2020). Extinction risk and threats to plants and fungi. *Plants, People, Planet, 2*(5). https://doi.org/10.1002/ppp3.10146

4   Friedlingstein, P., et al. (2020). Global carbon budget 2020. *Earth System Science Data, 12*: 3269–3340.

5   Salk Institute for Biological Studies (2019). *Harnessing the power of plants to capture and store enough carbon to slow climate change.* https://www.audaciousproject.org/grantees/salk-institute-for-biological-studies

6   UNEP (2021). *Becoming #GenerationRestoration: Ecosystem restoration for people, nature and climate.* United Nations Environment Programme.

7   The University of the West of England, Bristol, Science for Environment Policy: European Commission DG Environment News Alert Service, edited by SCU.

8   Farshid, A., et al. (2019). Urban green space cooling effect in cities. *Heliyon, 5*(4), 8 April. e01339. https://doi.org/10.1016/j.heliyon.2019.e01339

9   Manaia, J. P., Manaia, A. T., & Rodriges, L. (2019). Industrial hemp fibers: An overview. *Fibers, 7*(12): 106. https://doi.org/10.3390/fib7120106

10 FAO (2022). Livestock and landscapes: Sustainability pathways. https://www.fao.org/3/ar591e/ar591e.pdf

11 McDonald, J. (2019). Amazon doesn't produce 20% of Earth's oxygen. FactCheck.org, 3 September. https://www.factcheck.org/2019/09/amazon-doesnt-produce-20-of-earths-oxygen/

12 Ehrenberg, R. (2015). Global forest survey finds trillions of trees. *Nature* (2015). https://doi.org/10.1038/nature.2015.18287

CHAPTER 13

KEY MESSAGES

360　Remember to rest

Being part of the climate justice movement is not easy. There are many obstacles on the path to justice, including those in power who benefit from the status quo. But the movement cannot advance if the people who are part of it are exhausted.

The global system of capitalism is designed to extract the very most from different resources for the lowest price. Exploitation is baked into our economic system, which leaves both people and planet depleted and unable to recuperate.

In a system like this, resting is a rebellious act. Rest is fundamental to a happy and healthy life, and it can take many different forms:

- Physical rest means resting the body, including sleeping and taking part in physically nourishing activities like yoga or massage.
- Emotional rest means taking some time to journal, meditate, spend time in nature, or simply let your mind wander without any stimulation.
- Notice that none of these activities is profit-oriented or inherently 'productive'.
- Rest should not be a privilege available only to those who can afford it.

The movement to save the planet is also a movement to prioritize rest. To achieve a just and green future, we must prioritize rest – especially for marginalized people and for our exploited and depleted planet.

361　You don't have to be perfect to be in the movement

If there's one thing you can take away from reading this book, it's that you don't need to be perfect to be in the movement for climate justice.

Trying to be perfectly eco-friendly and expecting that same perfection from others only impedes progress from being made.

Any movement made up of humans is bound to be imperfect, because humans are imperfect, confusing and contradictory.

The exploitative system we live in allows only a privileged few to be perfect activists. In a system that's not designed with sustainability in mind, perfect sustainability can only be accessed by the most privileged. And that needs to change.

We need to go beyond judging ourselves and others based on whether we eat meat, use a reusable tote bag or avoid flying enough.

Instead, we should turn that judgement on governments that continue to allow companies to destroy our environment. On the oil and gas companies that have been funding climate denial for decades. On the fast-fashion companies that exploit their (mostly women) garment workers. On the politicians who serve the interests of profit over Indigenous peoples and planet.

Don't be discouraged if you can't do everything perfectly. Whoever you are, whatever you do, perfect or imperfect, the planet needs you in the movement.

362   How to engage family and friends on climate change

A huge part of activism is trying to get other people to care about the cause you're fighting for. There are a couple of important things to remember when trying to engage your friends and family on everything you've learned about the climate crisis.

People are won over by stories, not facts. When trying to engage people on issues you care about, it can be helpful to share the story of what moved you to get involved in the cause. Your personal story and the actions you personally take are more relatable and effective than cold, hard facts.

It can be helpful to approach these conversations with curiosity by asking questions about the other person's point of view. These questions can serve as tools of reflection – they might not get the person to change their mind in that instant, but they plant a seed that might change the person's outlook on the issue.

By asking questions, you begin to understand why the other party thinks the way they do, which means you can address their concerns or hesitations more effectively.

363 How to engage politicians on climate change

One of the most effective ways to take action on climate change is to get in touch with your local political representative.

In democratic countries, politicians represent the interests of their constituencies. When enough people from different constituencies reach out to politicians to voice their concerns about climate change, this issue becomes a priority in the government.

There is no one way to reach out to your local representative. Email them, tweet them, write letters, and be specific about the issues you care about and how they affect you.

Are you worried about food apartheid in your community? Do you think air pollution is getting out of hand? Tell your representative exactly what you would like them to do, and ask questions about how they are taking action on these issues.

Hopefully this book has given you the knowledge to be able to recognize problems and associated solutions in your community.

Never underestimate the value of letting your concerns be known to your local representative, especially if you have the privilege of living in a democratic country.

364   Ethical consumption versus consumer activism

To be an ethical consumer is to use your power as a consumer within an existing system to edge it towards being better.

Being an ethical consumer means voting for the kind of world you want with your wallet by supporting ethical local businesses, going plant-based, and buying cruelty-free and sustainable products. By doing this, you send a signal to the market that there is demand for sustainable, ethical products, and the market adjusts to accommodate for this demand. If enough people do this over a long period of time, the world can change for the better.

The problem with this approach alone is that we currently don't have the luxury of time. That's where consumer activism comes in.

Consumer activism means advocating for policy changes so the system can improve faster. It involves voting for politicians who prioritize citizens and the environment, campaigning for antitrust laws and garment worker protections, boycotting harmful companies, demanding that governments tax harmful goods, and making your concerns known to your local political representatives.

There have been many successful consumer activist movements that have brought swift change in many unjust corporations. The civil rights movement employed many elements of consumer activism in the United States, starting in the 1910s, when Black people started a 'Don't Buy Where You Can't Work' campaign, boycotting companies that practised racial discrimination in hiring.[1]

If you're wondering where to go from here, try combining both consumer activism and ethical consumerism into your daily life. Being an ethical consumer is a privilege because buying better for the planet and people is often more expensive. Being a consumer activist is something everyone can participate in. If you can do both – that's great!

365   The case for hope

Hope is a special feeling that can only be described as the belief that everything will turn out okay, no matter how hard present circumstances might be. The ability to have hope about complicated matters like climate change is uniquely human, which makes it uniquely powerful.

It is when we're armed with hope that we can persist in our struggle for justice, even when the prospects seem bleak. It is when we remember those who persevered, sacrificed and fought before us – civil rights leaders in the United States, Indigenous peoples from the Achuar people in Peru to the Dayak people in Borneo, the women of the Chipko movement, to name only a few – that we are given the motivation to carry on.

In the case of the climate crisis, many are waking up to the reality of the unjust system that has allowed corporations to exploit people and planet for too long. Younger generations have been profoundly shaped by the Coronavirus pandemic, racial unrest, unfettered inequality, and impending climate collapse. These young people are now growing into adults and getting their foothold in the world, and their influence is already bringing about change.[2]

We can also find hope when we look inwards. There are people like you who deeply care and want to make a difference, enough to pick up this book and learn how. We must never forget about ourselves and the power we each have to make a difference. The exploitative system we live in thrives when we lose hope and faith in ourselves and our communities.

There are plenty of reasons to have hope in the coming years. Personally, what gives me immense hope is the hundreds of people who make up the worldwide community of activists who are working tirelessly every day to spread awareness and education.

Think about what gives you hope, write it down and use it as your power and strength, as a reminder during the tough times that inevitably lie ahead.

References

1   Lightfoot, E. B. (2019). Consumer activism for social change. *Social Work*, *64*(4), 301–309.

2   Gray, G. (2020). The politically active generations: Millennials, Gen Z care about the debt – and more. www.americanactionforum.org/insight/the-politically-active-generations-millennials-gen-z-care-about-the-debt-and-more/, 7 February.

ACKNOWLEDGEMENTS

It is quite an impossible task to mention everyone who has influenced and inspired me on one page, so I'd like to extend my general and heartfelt thanks to all of my friends around the world, my extended family, and the Barnard community.

A few special mentions:

Firstly, I'd like to thank my mum, Vafa, who fought hard to give me every opportunity in life and gave me the courage to write this book.

I'd like to thank my dad, Robin, who taught me to never stop asking questions, and whose unrivalled sense of morality inspires me to always do the right thing.

I'd like to thank my grandparents, Fakhraddin and Dilshad, from whom I learned the power of community and the importance of integrity.

I extend my deepest gratitude to activists who dedicate their lives to educating and inspiring people like me, uncovering the truth, and fighting for a better future for our planet and its inhabitants.

Lastly, I'd like to thank my best friend Kwame from the bottom of my heart: I couldn't have gotten through the task of actually writing this book without you. Thank you for your unwavering support and patience, for being my shoulder to cry on when the world felt unsafe, for being my personal chef on long writing days, and for being my loudest cheerleader.

IT'S TIME TO SEIZE THE DAY.
ALL 365 OF THEM.

365 – your day-by-day guide to living better and working smarter

365 Ways to be More Stoic 978-1-52939-044-5

365 Ways to Develop Mental Toughness 978-1-52939-764-2

365 Ways to Save the Planet 978-1-52939-741-3

365 Ways to Live Mindfully 978-1-52939-039-1

365 Ways to Have a Good Day 978-1-52938-224-2